FORLORN HOPE

Colonel Thomas Rainborough
The Gardner drawing in the Sutherland Collection, illustrations for
Clarendon's History of the Great Rebellion. Original picture with the
Colonel's grandson at Rochester, U.S.A.

Ashmolean Library, Oxford.

FORLORN HOPE

*Soldier radicals of the
seventeenth century*

Antonia Southern

The Book Guild Ltd
Sussex, England

First published in Great Britain in 2001 by
The Book Guild Ltd
25 High Street,
Lewes, East Sussex
BN7 2LU

Typesetting in Times by
Keyboard Services, Luton, Bedfordshire

Printed in Great Britain by
Bookcraft (Bath) Ltd, Avon

A catalogue record for this book is
available from the British Library

ISBN 1 85776 519 2

For Hugo

CONTENTS

LIST OF ILLUSTRATIONS

ACKNOWLEDGEMENTS

I would like to express my gratitude to the staff of the following institutions: the London Library, the British Library, the British Museum, Dr Williams's Library, the Grocers' Company and the National Army Museum in London, the Public Record Office at Kew, the National Maritime Museum at Greenwich, the Bodleian and Ashmolean Libraries in Oxford, the Wiltshire County Council Library in Trowbridge and the Huntington Library in California, USA. My editors, Joanna Bentley and Sheila Lynford, have been unfailingly helpful and saved me from many blunders.

I received much help and encouragement from my former tutor, the late Dr Anne Whiteman, information on various subjects from the late Theo Mathew, *Windsor Herald*, from Major-General Sir Jeremy Moore and Dr Ian Roy. Sir William Dugdale allowed me access to the archives at Merevale and his daughter, Matilda May, found all the relevant documents for me. Mr John d'Arcy helped with the decyphering of a most difficult seventeenth-century hand, Mr and Mrs Henry Savill and Mr and Mrs Oliver Stephenson visited Colchester and Pontefract, respectively, on my behalf. The genesis of this book lies in fifty-year-old memories of a conversation with a most distinguished professional soldier. A much-decorated general, veteran of the Second World War, explained to a sixteen-year-old schoolgirl that soldiers were *always* on duty as servants of the State and that their duty of obedience was absolute. I am most grateful to Mr Ivor Blomfield for talking to me about his father and for confirming my impression of his attitude to soldiers in politics.

My particular thanks are reserved for Augusta and Philip Shirley, Humphrey and Emma Southern and Fanny and Jim Park: sternest of critics, most constant of supporters.

INTRODUCTION

There was war in heaven. (The Book of Revelation 12 v.7)

A sacrament is a soldier's oath, when we were baptized we took press money, and vowed to serve under the colours of Christ. (Simeon Ashe, 1642)

An English army entered the City of London in August 1647 and an English general, in civilian dress which can have deceived no one, took office as Head of State in December 1653. Since Cromwell, no English general has achieved, or aimed at, political office, except Wellington, who can scarcely be regarded as a politician with any sort of political creed. Wellington saw himself as a servant of the Crown: prepared to form a government if invited to do so by Queen Victoria, in the same way that he was prepared to do battle with her enemies in the field. Aggression was fashionable in the eighteenth and nineteenth centuries in England, represented by a naval figure, John Bull, and directed against foreigners rather than fellow-countrymen. Having an empire is a way of exporting war rather than experiencing it at home.

Since 1688 our civil quarrels have not been sufficiently bitter for appeal to the sword, and the army, homogeneous with the nation, has had no wish to interfere in politics. Westminster has not needed a Rubicon for the last three centuries. In the twentieth century wars have been fought by English armies with the greatest gallantry for ideals, to fulfil treaty obligations, to make the world safe for democracy. Our finest

1

soldiers have seen themselves as servants of the State, just as Wellington did, and armies in politics have been deplored; a principle which emerged from the seventeenth-century civil wars and the terrible, and, in English history, unique events referred to above. The Head of State in England is not head of the armed forces, and calling in the troops has been regarded as a positively last resort by governments faced with strikes or civil disorder in the last two hundred years. Civil and military affairs exist in separate compartments in this country.[1]

This is consistent with General Monck's 'principles'. After Oliver Cromwell's death, Monck smugly opined: 'Soldiers receive and observe commands but give none.' The issue of soldiers in politics was actually less clear-cut than this during the long and agonising period of civil disagreement which characterised the seventeenth century, a 'war without an enemy', when it could justly be held, as by Sexby, that 'every man is a soldier ... against common enemies, and those that are traitors to the Common-wealth.'[2]

Monck himself, a Royalist soldier of fortune who turned his coat at the right moment and became a Roundhead general, subsequently played a leading part in the politics of the restoration of the monarchy and the disassociation of the army from civil affairs, involving its disbandment. Pepys was sanguine about this disbandment. In 1663 he reported: 'of all the old army now you cannot see a man begging about the streets... You shall have this captain turned a shoemaker; the lieutenant a baker; this a brewer; that a haberdasher ... every man in his apron and frock as if they had never done anything else.' The soldiers of the New Model Army were citizen-soldiers: they seriously tried to adapt to peace and to believe that their victory in the field had been crowned by a just and lasting settlement. The careers of William Rainborough, Edward Sexby and Richard Rumbold, all survivors of victory in battle, show how sadly mistaken they were. Monck secured a fortune, a dukedom and employment as a 'General at Sea' under Charles II.[3]

The five subjects of this book were all volunteers in the New

Model Army; they could all claim with truth that they were not members of 'a mere mercenary army, hired to serve any arbitrary power of a state ... [but] took up arms in judgment and conscience ... to defend their own and the people's just rights and liberties'. None of them achieved fortune or fame other than posthumously. Only one died at liberty and in his bed – not in England. All were driven by the same conviction: a conviction that they were fighting for a settlement of the kingdom, including all its inhabitants, or, at any rate, a greater number of these than had previously been recognised as part of the political nation. They were a 'forlorn hope' in both senses of the term; on the one hand doomed to defeat as any minority invoking democratic procedures and, on the other hand, in the traditional military sense, as a picked troop leading an attack on a well-defended position. The ideals which excited and inflamed them in seventeenth-century England were eventually achieved without bloodshed. These ideals seem so commonplace today that they may even be taken for granted.[4]

The radicals of the 1640s wanted a written constitution, sovereignty of an annually elected parliament, the right to silence and legal representation for the accused, freedom of conscience and of debate, equality before the law, freedom of trade, the right to vote and the right to rebel when faced with tyranny. As a principle, they wanted freedom from conscription, the only item in their programme which has not been conceded in modern Britain.* (A written constitution remains under discussion.) They specifically upheld private property and denied the power of any elected Representative to 'make all things common'.[5]

The word 'radical' was not used in a political sense until the nineteenth century but political radicals did, in fact, exist, and from 1645 to 1649 were a visibly organised if heterogeneous party, with its centre in London and outlying groups in Essex, Kent, Buckinghamshire, Cambridgeshire and Hertfordshire.

---

*Conscientious objectors have been recognised since the beginning of the Second World War. Their lives during the First World War were horrible.

This party had a published programme, a membership paying regular dues and its own newspaper, *The Moderate*. Its colour changed from blue to sea-green after Thomas Rainborough's death, in deference to his sea-faring background. Like many political parties, this one was christened by its enemies: the Levellers, 'fal'sly so called' as members claimed. Regular meetings were held at the Windmill, Mouth and Nag's Head taverns in the City, and also in Southwark and Wapping. From the time of its inception in 1645, the New Model Army contained a radical element and during the year 1647 co-operation between the London Levellers and the soldiers developed.[6]

All the five heroes in this book were Londoners as well as volunteers, fighters rather than writers, whose reported speeches as well as their actions show that they were influenced, perhaps even convinced, by Leveller ideas. They are not a homogeneous group although two were brothers. They were essentially individuals, representative of that most eccentric feature of mid-seventeenth-century England: the fact that democratic ideas were then to be found in the army of all places. The functioning of an army requires instant obedience to a chain of command and the New Model was famous for its discipline in the field. In spite of this discipline, a few within this army did manage to keep before them the right true end of war. Remarkably, in that status-conscious time, some even recognised the rights and needs of social classes other than their own.

Seventeenth-century society was characterised as an 'inequality of states, orders and degrees', a view which was both obvious and orthodox at the time. Every man was known by his name and rank, recognisable by the clothes he wore and the games he was allowed to play. Football and bowls, for example, were prohibited for servants and labourers. Gentlemen were distinguished by their coats of arms and by the fact that they did not work. It was an offence for a working-man to walk abroad on a week-day without a sign of his profession. Shakespeare's Henry V said of the English casualties at Agincourt, a duke, an earl, a knight and an esquire, 'none else of name'. Clarendon commented on Parliament's losses at the second battle of Newbury: 'The officers of the enemy's side were never talked of being for the most part of no better families than their common soldiers.' After the siege of Colchester, Fairfax decided who was to be condemned by order of the Council of War and who was to be left to civil justice, on the basis that military execution was appropriate for 'persons ... more near the condition of soldiers of fortune and less eminent'.*[7]

Seventeenth-century poets recognised death as a leveller. It was not so seen in society generally. The College of Heralds laid down the rules for aristocratic funerals, the precise rank of the chief mourner – equal to the rank of the deceased – and the appropriate number of supporting mourners of lesser degree. Burial rites offset God's levelling judgement with a reassertion of rank and prestige on earth. In this context the funeral of trooper Robert Lockyer is the more remarkable.†[8]

The law operated in accordance with this view of society. Punishment fitted the criminal rather than the crime. 'No goods: to be whipped' was a frequent decision of JPs at quarter sessions. Benefit of the clergy, by which Ben Jonson escaped hanging, originally designed to protect the right of the clergy to be tried in ecclesiastical courts, operated to the advantage of the literate. Those convicted of a felony escaped death if they could read the 'neck verse' (Psalm 51, v.1.), a privilege which in 1623 was even extended to a woman. It was the same in civil actions. In 1641 the House of Commons in committee heard a dispute between Lord Mandeville and the tenants of Somersham concerning a drainage project. In theory the two were equal parties, in practice Lord Mandeville was given a seat and allowed to keep his hat on (a sign of rank), and the tenants stood bare-headed at the back of the room. In this social context the views of Rumbold, Sexby and

---

* In fact two gentlemen, Sir Charles Lucas and Sir George Lisle, were selected for summary punishment on this occasion. There were deemed to be special circumstances. The execution created an uproar. See p. 61.

† See p. 85.

the two Rainboroughs can be seen to be amazing and the published views of the civilian Leveller leaders, John Lilburne, William Walwyn and Richard Overton, truly revolutionary.[9]

Post-war defeat and disillusion drove many seventeenth-century radicals into pacifism. 'The Cause was too good to have been fought for ... Nature is at work and the world will not go the faster for our driving'. It drove others into crime. 'The Cause we had was very good though we ourselves were bad.' Three of the subjects in this book engaged in criminal activities: they cannot be described as *bad*. Their careers illuminate fifty-odd years of misfortune and desperate endeavour, which also happen to be fifty years of imagination and moral courage displayed by a minority, seldom equalled in English history and never surpassed before or since.[10]

Colonel Thomas Rainborough, not one of the criminals, was potentially the most influential of these five soldiers with a distinguished fighting career in the First and Second Civil Wars. He was the highest-ranking officer in the New Model to support the radicals. His premature death, arguably murder, eased the trickery of setting up a commission to try the King and achieving his execution *before* a political settlement had been agreed, an outcome the radical leaders had foreseen and feared.

Trooper Robert Lockyer was a Leveller martyr at the age of twenty-three after seven years' faithful service in the cause of Parliament, by all accounts a thoughtful and intelligent character as well as a brave man. He is a classic and tragic example of the impossibility of soldiers in politics, civilian soldiers, as so many of the New Model saw themselves.

Major William Rainborough had emigrated to New England and acquired some status there by 1640; he returned to fight for Parliament in 1642. He entered the political scene on his own account as an officer-agitator (agent, engaged in arguing the soldiers' cause) in 1647, supported his brother Thomas on occasion in the struggles of that year and tried to explain the issues to the men of his baffled regiment. He marched in the van of the demonstration at his brother's funeral and urged a search for the murderers. He served the Commonwealth and

Protectorate governments so far as he was allowed, clearly frustrated and opposed to aspects of these regimes. In 1660 he was accused of treason, escaping to New England on payment of a bond of £500 and dying there in the 1670s.

Edward Sexby enlisted as a trooper in the First Civil War and achieved the rank of colonel in 1650. He was a leading agitator in 1647 and served the Commonwealth and Protectorate governments in a military and diplomatic capacity. Finally, he turned against Cromwell, 'a Tyrant because he has no right to govern and because he governs tyrannically', became involved in attempts on the Protector's life and died in prison in consequence.

Richard Rumbold, like Sexby, was a trooper who was given a commission after the execution of the King. He had opposed the Grandees* in the Army in 1649, but subsequently been forgiven and re-instated, serving until the Army was disbanded after the Restoration. He risked a prosperous peacetime career because he found that he could not stomach the rule of Charles II or James II, became involved in active opposition to both and died on the scaffold, proudly claiming that he 'had been fighting against these idols of monarchy and prelacy since he was nineteen years of age'.

The outbreak of the Civil War in 1642 was as puzzling to contemporaries as it has subsequently proved to be to historians. What did the Royalists and Roundheads† think they were killing each other for? Changes in the law, achieved in 1641, had satisfied many of the King's critics. The Long Parliament was poorly attended when it re-assembled after the summer recess in October of that year. The Grand Remonstrance, a list of all the illegal and unpopular things the King's government had done in the 1630s, was out of date in

---

* Grandees, a pejorative term for Cromwell, Ireton and others among the high-ranking officers of the New Model, was coined by John Lilburne and increasingly used by all radicals.

† It goes without saying that the name 'Roundhead' in this book is not reckoned to be descriptive and does not imply a social sneer. It sometimes seems more euphonious than 'Parliamentarian'. Thomas Rainborough's hair, though apparently rather thin on top, curled on his shoulders, as did the hair of officers in the armies of both sides.

legal terms by November 1641 but vital, politically, if those who still distrusted Charles I were to maintain their position. It passed by only eleven votes after a division in the small hours, highly unusual in the seventeenth century. Swords were drawn over the proposal to publish it; 'to remonstrate downwards, to tell stories to the people, and talk of the King as of a third person'.[11]

Rebellion in Ireland in October 1641 had precipitated a crisis. An army was necessary to deal with this; yet some refused to trust the King, traditional and hitherto unquestioned head of the armed forces, with such power. An army could, all too easily, be turned against his enemies in England. Charles I, in fact, showed his willingness to resort to force in the typically bungled attempt to arrest the five members in the Commons, which unsuccessful *coup* led to his leaving his capital on 10th January 1642.

From that moment the emergence of two armed sides was a possibility. Hull was an arsenal and in April 1642, the King was refused entry to the town by the Governor, obeying orders, as he said, from Parliament. An Ordinance appealing for plate, money and horses for Parliament was issued in June, the same month as Commissions of Array were issued in the King's name under the Great Seal. Loyal JPs who received both these sets of orders must have been sorely perplexed. A skirmish over Parliament's Ordinance in July provided an occasion for bloodshed, the first blood to be shed in the Civil War. In August the King raised his standard at Nottingham. Against this background of a war in progress, peace negotiations continued up till 1645, and after the King's surrender in 1646, demonstrating the doubts of the Roundheads, unwilling aggressors in a fight against the established order.

'Religion was not the thing at first contested for ... [in the Civil War]'. Oliver Cromwell was right, of course. Religion does not primarily mean conduct of services in the Established Church or the issue of Church government. Both of these had been major sources of dispute between the King and his opponents in the 1630s and early 1640s. The first was settled by the Commons' Resolutions of September 1641, condemning high church practices such as railed-off altars, crucifixes, scandalous pictures of any member of the Trinity or the Virgin Mary and bowing at the name of Jesus. The second was the subject of the last act of the Long Parliament to secure royal assent: the Bishops' Exclusion Act whereby bishops were excluded from the House of Lords and all temporal authority. This act became law in February 1642. Archbishop Laud's 'Beauty of Holiness' had antagonised many during the Personal Rule of Charles I, largely because of its political aspect: the Laudian Church essentially stood for the union of Church and State. Its outward and visible signs were an obvious and easy target for its opponents but it was less easy to agree on what to put in its place. Unfinished business concerning the government of the Church and its liturgy was left to the Westminster Assembly of Divines, one hundred and twenty clerics and thirty members of the laity, later assisted by eight Scottish commissioners, ordered to begin their deliberations in July 1643. During the war, radical attitudes in religion developed apace and produced radical attitudes in politics.[12]

'God brought it [i.e. religion] to that in the end': this is how Cromwell's judgement, quoted earlier, continued. Religion certainly kept the soldiers on both sides fighting and Cromwell was not the only leader to recognise that men fight better when they are inspired. Royalist and Roundhead preachers were equally active in stirring up a fighting spirit and condemning neutral attitudes.

'Still a little before the Civil Wars, the ordinary sort of people were not taught to read. Nowadays books are common and most of the poor people understand letters; and the many good books and variety of turns of affairs have put all the old fables out of doors...' It has been estimated that only one man in five in the New Model Army was illiterate. In 1648 the Army had its own newspaper, *Mercurius Militaris*, followed in 1649 by *The Armies Modest Intelligencer*. Study of the Bible, the *Soldiers' Pocket Bible* produced in August 1643 and the *Soldiers' Catechisme* of 1644, combined with lay preaching and the fact that ministers who could not conform to the

Established Church might find employment as regimental chaplains under a sympathetic colonel, suggested new political attitudes in Parliament's armies.[13]

That radical politics in the seventeenth century had their genesis in radical religion is not surprising since religion was the framework of life in those days, the idiom in which all men thought. As always, in a society in which the Church is powerful and influential, there were anti-clericals, scoffers and blasphemers, to be distinguished from genuine questioners of the established order. There were also heretics – a sure sign of the vitality of belief – very few atheists (admittedly, admission of atheism would have been dangerous) and no recognisable agnostics (agnosticism is a nineteenth-century concept). Every facet of life came within the sphere of religion and those who were prepared to challenge the Established Church and its hierarchy found the State and society followed. The Bible, a dangerous and revolutionary book especially in the hands of the unlearned, suggested that all men and even all women were equal – or so the Baptists found. Toleration, described by a conservative as 'the grand design of the Devil, his masterpiece and chief engine', was essential to the radicals, allowing for progressive revelation and the operation of reason in conjunction with the Scriptures. Religious and political radicals eventually parted company because toleration, in the long run, involves toleration for sceptics as well as believers. Many religious radicals took refuge in pacifism and a belief in equality in the eyes of God rather than man.

The association of religious and political radicals may have lasted for a short time but it was a vitally important influence in the ideas of the latter. Richard Baxter, after a horrifying two years as a chaplain in the New Model, described his troopers: 'Many honest men of weak judgments and little acquaintance with such matters ... [were] ... seduced into a disputing vein ... sometimes for state-democracy, sometimes for church-democracy...' The war gave these ideas time to spread. The matter was sensitive, and authority, fearful and increasingly hostile, but the preachers could not be silenced and by 1647 the damage had been done. William Dell found a social message in Isaiah. He preached a sermon before the siege of Oxford which Thomas Rainborough could well have heard.

> A man that is a natural man, a sinful and unregenerate man ... though in this present world he may be a gentleman, or a knight, or a nobleman, or a King; yet in the eyes of God and his Saints, he is but a vile person; and a poor mean Christian that earns his bread by hard labour is by a thousand times more precious and excellent than he, according to the judgment of God and his Word.

This 'poor mean Christian ... a thousand times more precious' than his social superiors sounds like a forebear of the 'poorest he in England' of Thomas Rainborough's Putney speech when the Colonel could not find evidence for a propertied franchise in the Law of God. He may also be related to the man who was not born with a saddle on his back, ready for another, booted and spurred, to ride him, described by Richard Rumbold on the scaffold in 1685.[14]

The Rainboroughs and Robert Lockyer shared a common background of religious radicalism. The Rainborough brothers lived in Wapping from their youngest days (the family had moved there in the 1620s) and Wapping was a centre of nonconformity in the first half of the seventeenth century. Thomas Rainborough appointed a Baptist chaplain to his regiment in 1645. Robert Lockyer, aged sixteen, received adult baptism in Bishopsgate in 1642, the same year in which he enlisted in Parliament's army. Richard Rumbold was also a Baptist. Both he and Lockyer refused the consolation of the appointed chaplains at their respective executions, preferring to 'seek God in their own way'. Sexby was not one of the most religious of the Levellers but he made much use of Biblical imagery in his struggles with the Grandees. At Putney he told them that they were 'in a wilderness condition', the wilderness in the Old Testament signifying disorder and darkness. He reminded his accusers that God had left slaves with remedies against cruel masters when he justified the attempted murder of Cromwell as Protector.[15]

Surprising secular influences, encouraging soldiers of the New Model Army to consider new ideas, included the reading of classical texts. The soldiers of the New Model Army, many of them volunteers, were far from the brutal and licentious soldiery of legend. In 1668 Thomas Hobbes gave 'the reading of books of policy and history of the ancient Greeks and Romans' as a cause of the Civil War. In Hobbes's opinion, poorly educated fanatics had learned the wrong lessons from these sources. Livy, Tacitus and Plutarch were all available in translation in seventeenth-century England, and the theme of political power, claimed by, or appertaining to, citizen-soldiers runs through these authors. A pamphlet written in 1648 describes agitators, 'two of the most seditious common soldiers', negotiating with Scipio about their arrears of pay. At Putney, Thomas Rainborough showed himself well aware of the implications of the Grandees' use of the word 'democratic' as a criticism of the Leveller franchise. The Greeks had seen democracy as the worst form of government, leading to anarchy and mob rule, and he was quick to put up a defence against this charge.[16]

The answer was eventually to be consensus politics. Within two hundred and fifty years, the aims of the Levellers were achieved without bloodshed and for this there is much cause to be thankful. The defeat of the Levellers in the seventeenth century is to be deplored; it was followed by a time of oppression and neglect of the poor seldom, if ever, equalled in English history.

Any one of these five men might have claimed that consensus politics were for Laodiceans, luke-warm ideas were only fit to be spat out. They represented, in their own time, a 'revolutionary civilizing force' and their story may be taken as a memorial for the many who perished without one in their own time.[17]

PART 1

Thomas Rainborough c.1610–1648

The poorest he in England hath a life to live as the greatest he. (Thomas Rainborough, Putney, 1647)

Before 1639, when he married a Miss Margaret Cole in Ipswich, nothing is known for certain about the life of Thomas Rainborough, not even the date of his birth.[1] By the time he had reached his thirties, and a measure of fame, he was, according to his portrait, a burly, handsome man of great physical strength (also attested by his choice of the pike as his weapon) and proven courage. He was a man of action, a doer rather than a talker, who found negotiating less congenial than fighting but was, nonetheless, prepared to sit on committees, and even to compromise – after passionate argument. At Putney, in October 1647, he explained how much more he valued command of his regiment than his seat in the Commons.

He may have attended grammar school but clearly had not a great deal of formal education. There would not have been time for this if, as seems probable, he went early to sea, 'bred to the sea and the son of an eminent commander', as Clarendon describes him. In the late 1640s he was lampooned in the Royalist press as 'the Skipper's Boy', and described, admiringly, in the 1690s as an Admiral who had started life as a cabin boy. It was usual in the first half of the seventeenth century to serve, as Thomas Rainborough did, as he was ordered, indiscriminately on land or at sea. Only during the later Commonwealth period did it come to be recognised that

13

seamen were less prone to accidents than 'Gentlemen Captains' and the command 'Left Wheel' could cause mirth among sailors. In the First Civil War, Thomas Rainborough emerged as an imaginative and practical soldier, an expert in siege warfare and a colonel with the wit to devise a new order of battle, sufficiently impressive to be worth a whole chapter in a military text-book published in 1650.[2]

Evidence of Thomas Rainborough's proclaimed motive for taking up arms in the Civil War can be found at an early stage in the proceedings from his personal standard.* (See Fig. 3) Officers of the rank of captain and above had a free hand in designing their colours and choosing their mottoes in English armies of the seventeenth century. Banners in large armies distinguished troops of different nations; in smaller bodies they distinguished those of different leaders in order that the commander-in-chief could assess the behaviour of each corps. Of course they were also vitally important as a rallying point for soldiers scattered in the progress of an action. Records, water-colour drawings, of Civil War banners were most carefully preserved because contemporaries recognised their significance. They are a clue to the mind of many officers as to what they thought they were fighting for. They provided visible propaganda for the fighting men in each troop or regiment when the colour was paraded in order that it should be easily recognised. Its message could be explained and used as an inspiration – particularly important when pressed men were involved.

Thomas Rainborough's colour demonstrates militant Protestantism of a kind which would be deplored in the twenty-first century: a mailed fist, clutching a flaming sword, emerges from a cloud which also houses a book, *Verbum Dei*, the Word of God. Above is the motto *Vincit Veritas*, the Truth Conquers. Below is the Moor's head, appropriated by the Rainboroughs as their family seal after Thomas Rainborough's father had successfully rescued nearly three hundred English-

---

*The attribution of this colour to Colonel Thomas Rainborough is controversial. An analysis of the evidence is to be found in Appendix A.

men, prisoners of pirates off the coast of Algeria, in 1637. (It was usual for colonels of foot to use their family badge on their standard if they did not have a crest.) The allegation that Rainborough's regiment was one of the 'chiefest praying and preaching regiments in the army' in 1645 and that Colonel Rainborough was a 'professed Independent'* accords with evidence of his banner. In 1647 he could find no evidence in the law of God for a propertied franchise.[3]

He was never intimidated by position or rank, as is demonstrated over and over again in his dealings with the King and with Cromwell. He believed above all in the individual, endowed by God with reason, expected to make use of it, and entitled, insofar as the seventeenth century could conceive of these, to equal rights. The defects of his qualities included a degree of political naïvety, a tendency to act impulsively and to lose his temper. More than once in his career he was outwitted. He was uncertain in the realms of political theory – in spite of having such sound instincts. His career was too short to allow a really satisfactory estimate of his talents. The generosity and originality of his attitude to his fellow-men shines out of his speeches at Putney which have so fortunately survived.

Although he did not start from nowhere, Thomas Rainborough had to make his own way in the world – as did his brother William. They inherited money from their father in February 1642 and invested £1,000 jointly in April of that year in the Irish Adventure, a gigantic speculation in Irish land, a privatisation of the suppression of rebellion in Ireland which had broken out in October 1641. Thomas put up a further £500 in July 1642. Fellow subscribers included John Pym (£1,800),

---

* Presbyterians and Independents were the groups into which Parliamentarians divided, the former believing in a coercive State Church to which all should conform, the latter believing in the freedom of individual conscience, an existing division which hardened with the conclusion of the Covenant in September 1643. This divide in religion came to mirror a divide in politics, many Independents proving to be radical while Presbyterians became increasingly conservative.

Oliver Cromwell (£2,059) and the Royalist Sir Nicholas Crisp (£7,201). The investment was thought to be a good one. One thousand acres in Leinster were available for £600, in Munster for £450 and in Connaught and Ulster, respectively, for £300 and £200. Good land, no bogs, barren moors or forests, was specified, to be confiscated from all four provinces not just the most rebellious. Ulster, where the trouble had started, was regarded as containing the poorest land; economic considerations clearly took precedence over moral ones so far as confiscation was concerned in spite of the generous amount of pamphlet literature justifying the scheme. This looks like, and, in fact, *is* the unacceptable face of Puritanism, but the scheme by which Ireland was 'settled', after Cromwell's conquest in 1649, actually dates from 1642 and marks the last act of cooperation between King and Parliament. Charles I gave his assent to *The Act for the speedy and effectual reducing of the Rebels* on 19th March and this recognised shareholders, the Adventurers as they were called, who included future Royalists and future Roundheads. (It is true that the latter predominated and the subsequent truce between Charles I and the Irish rebels might have been foreseen.)[4]

In June 1642, the same month in which the King's Commissions of Array – the call to arms which answered Parliament's demand for money, plate and horses to preserve peace and liberty – were issued, a committee of fifteen Adventurers, including Thomas Rainborough, launched an expedition against the Irish rebels. Ten ships left Dover on 1st July 1642.

The fleet was commanded by Captain Benjamin Peter of the *Speedwell*; Thomas Rainborough, captain of the *Zantman*, was described as Vice-Admiral under him. They were accompanied on the expedition by Thomas's brother, William, and Benjamin's half-brother, Hugh (subsequently one of the regicides), both of whom had recently returned from New England because of the political situation in the mother country. Hugh Peter served as chaplain to the Adventurers' force and subsequently wrote an account of it, claiming that many Irish towns had been fired, rebels killed and corn burnt. He said that many

16

English had been relieved in forts and castles. Thomas Rainborough could not have been personally involved in this because he was serving continuously at sea, guarding the coast from Kinsale almost to Londonderry, preventing the landing of ships with supplies and reinforcements for the Irish.[5]

The brutality of service in Ireland revolted men of every political persuasion. Edmund Verney, an experienced soldier who had seen service in Scotland and the Netherlands, Royalist son of the King's Standard Bearer killed at Edgehill, wrote bitterly from Trim: 'We put some four score men to the sword (after casualties to their own side of twenty-three dead and thirty wounded) but, like valiant knights errant, gave quarter and liberty to all the women.'[6]

Arguments had been produced in favour of the Adventurers – that they intended to help fellow-Protestants, to spread the Gospel and demolish Antichrist, to help England, to make money, to assist younger sons, to replant Ireland with Protestants and to set up a Godly ministry there. These arguments are reminiscent in many ways of those produced in 1629 to justify the intended plantation of New England under John Winthrop. In both cases there is reference to Antichrist and the importance of spreading the Gospel (Protestant, understood). The New England adventurers maintained that the whole earth is the Lord's garden, a whole continent should not lie waste without improvement, nor savage people ramble over much land without title and that which is common to all is proper to none. They blandly asserted that there was more than enough for all. Property rights of the native Irish were adjudged forfeit by their disobedience. There is not much to choose between these two views. By 1649 an admittedly tiny minority was more enlightened. The Leveller William Walwyn was accused of saying then:

> That the sending over Forces into Ireland is for nothing else but to make way by the blood of the Army to enlarge their territories of power and Tyranny. That it is an unlawful War, a cruel and bloody work to go to destroy the Irish Natives for their Consciences (though they have killed

17

many thousand Protestants for their Consciences) and to drive them from their proper and native rights.

and that:

The cause of the Irish Natives in seeking their just freedoms, immunities and liberties, was the very same with our cause here, endeavouring our own rescue and freedom from the power of oppressors.

In 1647 soldiers of the New Model Army refused service in Ireland on a forcible rather than a voluntary basis, divorced from their own officers. The moral justice of fighting there was queried in a pamphlet of 1649 designed to be read by 'every Honest Officer to his soldiers and by the soldiers, one to another'. Thomas Rainborough was dead by then. It is impossible to say how or whether his own attitude to Ireland would have changed. It is legitimate to assume that he would have listened carefully to the views of his political allies and fellow-soldiers.[7]

As the Irish expedition was preparing to sail in June 1642, a struggle between King and Parliament developed over control of the navy. Rival Lords High Admiral were appointed and the quickness of Robert Rich, second Earl of Warwick, son of Penelope Rich (Philip Sydney's Stella), secured the fleet for the Roundheads. Those captains who refused to obey him were removed from their commands. These included Captain Kettleby of the *Swallow*, who was actually overpowered by his own men, and whose ship was then handed over to Thomas Rainborough. Control of the navy by Parliament ensured that the civil wars of the seventeenth century were confined to the British Isles and fought between British people. From the beginning the King and Queen ceaselessly negotiated for reinforcements and supplies – from the King of Denmark, Charles I's uncle, and from the Prince of Orange, his son-in-law – but for the most part these could not be landed. (An exception was Henrietta Maria herself, the 'She-Generalissima', who did successfully land on the coast of Yorkshire in March 1643, having crossed from Holland with supplies.) Thomas Rainborough, promoted by June 1643 to the *Lion*, a bigger and better-armed ship than the *Swallow*, captured a Scottish ship out of Leith, bound for Newcastle with Irish and Scottish troops to support the King. In the *Lion* he took part in a crucial engagement at Hull.[8]

As well as being an arsenal, Hull was a strategically important port where troops from Denmark might be landed and, therefore, a continuing anxiety even after the magazine had been safely sent to the Tower. The Governor, Sir John Hotham, appointed by Parliament, who had refused entry to the King himself in April 1642, later regretted his action. He wrote to the Speaker about three weeks before the battle of Edgehill, saying that he had no wish for either King or Parliament to be absolute conquerors. He expressed a fear that 'the necessitous people ... will presently rise in mighty numbers ... to the utter ruine of all the Nobility and Gentry of the kingdome.' By June 1643 there was serious fear that he and his son would surrender the town.[9]

The successful defence of Hull by the Roundheads involved operations by sea and on land. The *Lion*, commanded by Thomas Rainborough, accompanied by an armed merchantman with 500 infantrymen on board, arrived on 5th October to help the Fairfaxes (who had recently arrived in the city themselves). The landing was successful; Rainborough and his sailors (the complement of the *Lion* was 170 men) acquitted themselves well and Rainborough was rewarded, probably by Lord Fairfax himself, with the rank of colonel and command of 500 musketeers in the land battle which took place six days later on 11th October. Rainborough's servant was killed and his own life feared for but, in the event, he had been taken prisoner. Within less than a month, in response to a petition of his wife Margaret, he was exchanged for Captain Kettleby, his predecessor as Captain of the *Swallow*, a prisoner of Parliament for the past year. Exchange of prisoners fortunately became commonplace in the English civil wars. Hull was saved and remained in Parliament's hands for the rest of the war. The treacherous Hothams were sent to London for trial.[10]

From October 1643 till March 1645 Thomas Rainborough served in East Anglia, an area which was important on account of its commercial and agricultural wealth and its connections with London and the Netherlands. It was strategically important, too, in view of a possible Royalist advance from the north. Traditionally it was a centre of Puritanism, of zeal in matters of religion, sufficient, within the last twenty years, to produce the bulk of those emigrants driven into exile by the ritual conformity demanded by Archbishop Laud and his fellows. Four men from New England, described as 'the best military men in the colony', returned to take service in Rainborough's regiment, attracted by the fact that the commanding officer's name was known to them (through the Winthrop circle and those Rainboroughs who had emigrated) or by the idea of serving in an area which they knew.

The army of the Eastern Association was the precursor of the New Model, and many of those important in the fighting and politics of the future are to be found in its ranks. The Earl of Manchester, formerly Speaker of the House of Lords, a man of whom many spoke highly (although 'known meeknesse and sweetnesse of disposition' scarcely suggests a military leader), became major-general, with Oliver Cromwell as his second-in-command. This army numbered, on paper at least, 20,000 men. John Lilburne was colonel of a regiment of dragoons, and Edward Sexby a trooper in Cromwell's regiment. Thomas Rainborough's infantry regiment was on permanent garrison duty in Lincolnshire and he therefore missed taking part in the battle of Marsten Moor in July 1644. Garrison duty was no sinecure, however, in view of the constant threat of Royalist attacks from Newark, a borough which belonged territorially to the Queen and was full of inhabitants who were loyal to the sovereign lady of the manor.[11]

It cannot have been easy for Colonel Rainborough to maintain order in his regiment, with few occasions for excitement during the desperately wet summer and autumn of 1644. Morale was notoriously low among the infantry rank-and-file, whose pay was low and whose social origins, insignificant. Many had taken up arms for plunder rather than belief in a cause. The ratio of pressed men to volunteers rose to 50:50. It was fortunate that the regiment was a praying and preaching one. Radical religion contributed to the fighting spirit of the men and gave them an idea of what they might be fighting for.[12] In December 1644 the regiment was successful in taking Crowland, thought to be the key to the fen country, where a tiny body of Cavaliers had been holding out for two months against vastly superior Roundhead forces. This success was undoubtedly exaggerated by a partisan contemporary historian at a time when the fortunes of his side were low. An amphibious operation, such as Rainborough was well able to master-mind, resulted in a blockade and the surrender of the besieged, who had been living on roots and without salt for sixteen days. 'Valiant and virtuous Colonel Rainborough' became a much talked of and, in some Parliamentarian circles, popular man.[13]

By the end of 1644 war-weariness was evident throughout the country, although no realistic person could have hoped for much from the peace negotiations, known as the Treaty of Uxbridge, in progress throughout January and February. Both sides had recourse to pressing troops. A win-the-war party emerged among the Parliamentarians, initially divided over religion, dedicated, in the first place, to improving organisation of the war effort and countering the effects of increasing social conservatism and fear of victory. In January 1642 Parliament had appointed a Committee of Public Safety, succeeded, when the Scots entered the war, by a Committee of Both Kingdoms (later known as the Derby House Committee after its usual meeting-place). The generals Essex, Manchester and Waller were members of this committee, and so was

Cromwell from February 1644, but because they were usually with the armies, the working core in London was a quorum of civilians, subordinate to Parliament and bound to take its orders. Local organisation was in the hands of county committees, notoriously unwilling to operate outside their own immediate neighbourhood. The planning of pitched battles was virtually impossible and the job of the commander in the field eminently unsatisfactory. A plan was made to 'new-model' the army in terms of finance, commanding personnel and chain of command. What resulted was one of the most surprising institutions in English history.

Five months elapsed between December 1644, when the Lords first agreed to the raising of a new army with a new chain of command, and April 1645, when the Self-Denying Ordinance was finally passed. The birth-pangs of 'The Army of Parliament under the command of Sir Thomas Fairfax', nicknamed the 'New Model', or, by Charles I, the 'New Noddle', were painful. Fairfax was appointed General, Sir Philip Skippon, Major-General of Foot, while the post of Lieutenant-General in command of the Horse was, for the time being, left vacant. Thomas Rainborough was appointed Colonel of the 7th regiment of Foot, an amalgamation of three regiments from Manchester's army. Infantry regiments in the New Model were larger than previous regiments and there were therefore redundancies among infantry colonels, 240 of these to be precise. Rainborough clearly owed his place to Fairfax's confidence in his military ability.[14] He nearly lost it on account of his reputation for religious radicalism. His nomination was contested first in the Commons and then, more strenuously, in the Lords, together with that of his brother, William, and many others. The Commons eventually accepted Fairfax's list and sent repeated messages to the Lords in March 1645 to hurry up with the business. The Lords finally passed the list by one vote only. Lord Saye and Sele, a believer in 'win-the-war' and a supporter, therefore, to this extent, of the radicals, used a proxy vote for the Earl of Musgrove, Fairfax's grandfather, an Armada veteran and 'not able to be present'![15]

22

'Never did hardly any army go forth with less confidence of their own side, or more contempt of their enemies.' It was, however, rapidly and boldly equipped with scarlet uniforms (an inheritance from the Eastern Association army), horses and weapons. Throughout the month of April it was drilled and disciplined at Windsor before the major part of it was sent westward to relieve the siege of Taunton. Colonel Rainborough and his regiment were quartered at Abingdon with orders to watch over the King and Prince Rupert who were rumoured to be planning to leave Oxford and march north against the Scots. He was ordered to besiege Gaunt House outside Oxford and secured its surrender two weeks before the battle of Naseby.[16]

Naseby was Thomas Rainborough's first experience of a pitched battle, as was the case with many of his men. In the event it was an overwhelming Roundhead victory. Defeat would have been a disgrace in view of their superiority in numbers but the Army had only been in being for six weeks. It had no tradition as a fighting unit. The cavalry was made up of seasoned troopers, including the original Ironsides, but the infantry was an unknown quantity. On the day the right wing of horse under Cromwell was immediately successful; Ireton, on the left wing, lost half his horse to Prince Rupert who was then unable to halt and re-form his men for a second attack. The position in the centre, where an infantry battle was raging, was crucial and the Roundhead infantry were hard-pressed until Fairfax called up his reserves which included Rainborough's regiment. These reserves, according to Joshua Sprigge, historian of the New Model and one of Fairfax's chaplains, made a vital contribution to the eventual victory.

Royalist losses were enormous. So many officers were captured that the King could never have put another army in the field even if men could have been recruited, although this was not necessarily recognised by either side at the time. Naseby was a turning point, the beginning of a great course of victories for the New Model army, though the First Civil War dragged on for another ten months.[17] In the field there remained the Royalist armies of Goring and Hopton in the West, Montrose in Scotland and a number of fortified towns and country houses spread about in England. After negotiating the surrender of Leicester on 17th June, Thomas Rainborough's service was concentrated in the south-west; he took part in the battle of Langport and the sieges of Bridgwater and Sherborne, in which two of his junior officers were shot dead and given military funerals. At the siege of Bristol, the second city in the kingdom, held by the Royalists since 1643, the courage and tenacity of his regiment was especially commended by Cromwell himself. 'Colonel Rainborough ... had the hardest task of all at Priors-Hill-Fort ... and fought near three hours for it ... two hours at push of pike'.[18] Before Bristol, Thomas Rainborough had commanded the siege of Nunney Castle near Frome; after Bristol he went on to storm Berkeley Castle. From December 1645 he and his regiment were quartered in Abingdon after unsuccessfully besieging Corfe Castle, which did not surrender until April 1646.

The winter of 1645–46 was awful: the Thames froze, as it did fourteen times in the seventeenth century. Rainborough's regiment clearly found winter quarters in Abingdon tedious after the hectic activity of the past few months. The Governor of the town wrote crossly to the two Houses in February, asking them to order the officers of Colonel Rainborough's regiment to return and look to their charges. Apparently only four out of ten commanders were present. The Committee of Both Kingdoms empowered Colonel Rainborough to 'execute Martial law and punish by death offences contrary to the Laws and Ordinances published by Essex' so far as his own regiment and certain lately regimented companies of foot were concerned. The famous discipline of the New Model depended on constantly watchful administration; there was nothing new in the rules against plundering except that they were conscientiously enforced and it was only this, as had been shown in the West, which reconciled a neutral or Royalist local population to the presence of Parliament's soldiers.[19]

Colonel Rainborough's regiment assisted in the December blockade of Oxford and, in April 1646, it was put in charge of a line drawn from the Isis to the Cherwell, south of the city. The King actually escaped secretly but without difficulty over Magdalen Bridge in the east on 27th April and arrived at the Scots' headquarters in Southwell on 5th May. He had earlier been considering his options, the parties with whom he might treat: the English Parliament at Westminster, the Scots or the Independents, 'a faction newly grown up and with which he (the King) was utterly unacquainted', as Clarendon described them. Charles I had infinite confidence in his own power to charm and boundless confidence in his country's need of him. He sent emissaries to Colonel Rainborough at Woodstock asking for a safe conduct to London in order that he might negotiate in person there. He also asked for a guarantee that he would remain King, promising, in return, that Woodstock and other garrisons would be surrendered. Thomas Rainborough described these proposals in a letter to the Speaker and took no action himself. He was as well aware as others of the danger of divide and rule: 'These *indirect* addresses hinder the Proceedings of Parliament for Peace in a right way.' Oxford yielded on 24th June without a battle and Thomas Rainborough was then sent to take over command of the siege of Worcester which surrendered to him within three weeks of his appointment. One month later he was made Governor of the city, 'at the earnest desire of the Committee and gentlemen of the shire by reason of his discreet carriage in the taking of the city', as Fairfax wrote to the House of Commons. He has been 'very faithful, valiant, and successful in many undertakings since you put him under my command', the General went on to say – probably without intending to be sarcastic or make a point despite the Commons' reluctance, eighteen months earlier, to entrust Rainborough with the command Fairfax had wanted for him.[20]

Joshua Sprigge later listed the engagements of the New Model Army from April 1645 to August 1646, fifty-five in all. He gave statistical details of each action, including the name of the commander-in-chief on each occasion. Thomas

Rainborough was in command five times, as compared with Fairfax twenty-nine times, and Cromwell eight. No other officer commanded more than two engagements. He had played a leading part in the winning of the First Civil War.[21]

Some time after his appointment as Governor of Worcester, Thomas Rainborough was 'recruited' as Member of Parliament for Droitwich, a neighbouring borough. 'Recruiting' to the Commons to replace Royalist members who were deemed to have forfeited their seats had been going on spasmodically since August 1645. The war party at Westminster was searching for men with national, rather than local, interests who could be relied on to act bravely in the struggle for a settlement of the kingdom. Since 1642 Droitwich had been in the hands of a carpet-bagger, Endymion Porter, courtier, poet, friend and patron of poets, another carpet-bagger might prove acceptable and Thomas Rainborough had earned an excellent reputation as Governor of the city of Worcester. The electorate, generally, was war-weary and soldiers tended to be rejected as MPs in areas in which they had been fighting. Rainborough's success was a personal triumph as well as a victory for the war party. Elected in his middle thirties, he could have looked forward to a long period in the Commons, following the political tradition established by his father, if this hope had not been cut short by his murder.[22]

In February 1647, Thomas Rainborough took the oath to the Covenant of September 1643, as he was required to do on becoming a member of the Commons. This oath involved swearing that he would pursue 'the reformation of religion ... according to the Word of God, and the example of the best reformed Churches.' The Covenant had been a condition of the alliance between Parliament and the Scots. It became a symbol of the divisions developing between Parliament's supporters and soldiers. In the first place, Scottish and English conceptions of Presbyterianism differed fundamentally, the Scots favouring dominance of the clergy, the English, dominance of the laity; in the second place, the English were divided between Presbyterians and Independents. An increasing number of Englishmen were reacting against any form of coercive religious settlement. The sinister similarity between Old Priest and New Presbyter was observed. As an Independent Rainborough would not have liked the Covenant. He dodged taking it as an officer in the New Model Army when it was not strictly enforced. By the time he did take the oath as a Member of Parliament the wording had been shown to be as ambiguous as the original canny Independent negotiator, Sir Harry Vane, had intended and the promise one to which all Protestants could subscribe.[23]

From February to May 1647 Thomas Rainborough stayed in Westminster 'rather a sollicitor for, than the Colonel of [his] regiment, showing from time to time, the wants of his necessitous soldiers' as he later explained.[24] The political situation during these three months was becoming increasingly bitter and complicated and, like others, Thomas Rainborough had to decide where his loyalties lay and where his energies could best be spent.

He was not convinced that fighting action was over. He planned an expedition to Jersey to secure the island and the person of the Prince of Wales who had been living there for the last year. This expedition was eventually approved by Parliament; money and supplies were voted and Rainborough was formally appointed commander. (The Lords had demurred and put forward the name of a sound Presbyterian and 'French speaker' but they were overruled.) Rainborough's regiment was quartered in Hampshire in May 1647, ready to embark when notice should be given.[25]

From the point of view of Parliament this expedition was of minor importance. The members were preoccupied with the need to disband the expensive and possibly dangerous army. A 'neat plan', as it has been called, a cunning move on the part of the Presbyterians in Parliament, was put forward; the infantry of the New Model were to be disbanded, none to be kept in pay except a few garrisons, the cavalry reduced to a home establishment of 5,400 only, with 1,000 dragoons. A force was to be selected from the New Model to serve in Ireland under new officers. This was palpably intended to break the New Model as an entity. Except for Fairfax, there was to be no officer in the new army who had held rank above colonel in the old, none were to be MPs and all were to conform to the form of church government settled by Parliament – a much stiffer requirement than the Covenant which had been proved to be so elastic. Thomas Rainborough, in company with others, would have had to choose between his military and parliamentary careers.[26]

The Army's reaction to this plan was one of horror. Service in Ireland was unpopular, money for subsistence and pay there was even more uncertain than in England. It was reckoned unjust that men who had volunteered for service in England should then be drafted overseas. The soldiers were appalled at the idea of being separated from their old officers and concerned about such vital matters as the lack of an indemnity for war crimes like horse-stealing, no security for arrears of pay or provision of money to pay for quarters, and no provision for widows, orphans or the disabled. It cannot be denied that they had a point. They only had to quote *The Catechisme*, composed for Parliament's Army in 1644:

Q. How ought souldiers to be incouraged and rewarded?
A. They ought to be well-maintained, with sufficient allowance, for no man goeth on warfare at his own charge.
A. They that have received any hurt or losse by the warres, ought to be liberally provided for, and comfortably maintained all their dayes, *by them that sent them forth.**[27]

Accordingly, some of the soldiers circulated a petition for signature among their number. This petition listed the essential five points which concerned the Army: an indemnity against

---

* My italics.

criminal proceedings, security for arrears before disbandment, provision for the disabled, widows and orphans, money to pay for quarters (the soldiers were well aware of the burden they themselves inflicted on the public) and an admission that no volunteer should be compelled to serve outside the kingdom. They followed this up with an *Apologie*,[28] addressed to their officers, explaining their need to petition Parliament with their grievances and pointing out that, in the matter of arrears of pay, there was little difference between the situation of officers and men. The Army's petition was in the hands of the Commons by the end of the month of March. It inspired a Member of Parliament* to describe the soldiers as 'enemies of the State and Disturbers of the public peace', a monstrous description later known as 'the Declaration of Dislike'.[29]

The Army consistently claimed that they were citizens in arms, soldiers but also subjects with the rights of subjects. They supposed that they should not be deprived of 'the common privileges which every Englishman is born unto'. It is amazing and disgraceful that those for whom they had been fighting ignored their practical and reasonable anxieties. What was at stake for the people concerned was not a handout: it was money earned by the fighting men who had won the war for Parliament. Arrears of pay were a particularly serious matter for an infantryman, perhaps one hundred miles from home, who would have needed one month's pay at the statutory 8d per day simply to get there. Lack of an indemnity was serious for the cavalry; the punishment for having stolen or 'requisitioned' a horse was hanging. The City had already lent £200,000 for paying off the New Model and launching the Irish expedition. They would doubtless have gladly lent more

---

*This MP, Denzil Holles, had been a leading member of the opposition to Charles I in the early years of the Long Parliament, one of the Five Members spirited away to the City to avoid arrest by the King in person in January 1642. He subsequently became a leading member of the Presbyterian, or peace-party, in the Commons and, by 1647, a violent opponent of the Army. Using most intemperate language, he accused the soldiers of violence. He said they were no more than mercenaries, concerned solely about their arrears of pay. He was one of the eleven MPs the Army was determined to impeach in July 1647, whose escape to France was assisted by Vice-Admiral Batten, dismissed and replaced by Thomas Rainborough in September of the same year.[30]

in order to get rid of the New Model which they greatly feared. An initial four months' arrears would have satisfied the soldiers – on the evidence of Fairfax's foot regiment who offered to disband for this. Instead the New Model Army was demonised by Holles, alienated by the meanness of Parliament's treatment and ready for an alliance with articulate civilian radicals outside Parliament.[31]

Reaction in the Army was rapid in March 1647 because the experience of fighting together, living together, praying and arguing together, away from the traditions of their separate localities and civilian callings, had made the New Model a very much more sophisticated body than the collection of units and individuals assembled under one authority in April 1645. They had read pamphlets, or listened to other people reading them, and heard sermons which opened their minds. They had discussed 'Church democracy' and 'State democracy'. Among the 'errors' rampant in the Army, noted in February 1646 by a Presbyterian critic, most of them religious, was the idea that 'The People may call Parliament to account'. They may, in the next few months, have proved themselves 'young Statesmen', inexperienced in the 'little known art of statising' but some of them were ready to organise and to attempt to influence a settlement of the kingdom for which they had been fighting.[32]

Civilian radicals, the Leveller leaders, had drawn up a programme in the form of a petition, which came into the hands of the Commons a week before they got hold of the Army petition. This programme was concerned with wide issues, in contrast to the specific ones which were so understandably worrying the soldiers; the powers of the King and the House of Lords, the question of religious freedom, including abolition of tithes, and freedom to preach 'in a peaceable way', and reform of the law, including provision for proceedings in English and the principle that no accused was to be required to incriminate himself. There were social clauses too: a condemnation of the misery of begging and the farce of imprisonment for debt. Calling people names such as 'Roundhead' was declared to be an evil. The methods of soldiers and civilians were similar. The two petitions had been circulating,

30

canvassing for signatures, the one in London and the other in the Army, at the same time. In addition, connection between a Leveller leader and a future organiser in the Army had been made.*[33]

John Lilburne, one of the Leveller leaders, was, as usual, with him, in prison in the spring of 1647 but not cut off from the outside world. In the Tower, towards the end of 1646, he was allowed visitors if they would give their names to his jailor. These included 'some straggling soldiers' and 'men's wives'. In March 1647, he was visited by a 'knowing man out of the Army', most probably Edward Sexby who, as a cavalry trooper, would have had independent mobility. Another leading Leveller, Richard Overton, produced a pamphlet in April, defending the Army and answering those who were demanding its summary disbandment. 'It is evident ... that our just rights and liberties are now in more hazard than they were at first. This Army deserves our gratitude: its wishes are reasonable.'[34]

A committee was appointed by the House of Commons to examine the soldiers' petition and discover how it was circulated in the New Model. Thomas Rainborough was one of the members of this committee, a large one of diverse political membership including Cromwell and Ireton as well as the republican, Henry Marten, and the Presbyterians, William Strode and Denzil Holles himself. It advised that an ensign be imprisoned and that Colonel Robert Lilburne, brother of John and colonel of one of the most divided regiments in the Army, be sent for and examined, together with two other officers. Others in the Commons were not prepared to delay: the disbandment plan was finally voted on 25th May, to take place during the first fortnight in June, and the three officers were discharged without examination.[35]

Commissioners had been sent by the Commons to Fairfax's headquarters, then in Saffron Walden, to placate the Army so far as the proposed disbandment and service in Ireland were concerned. Rainborough did not attend these meetings in

---

* See p. 119.

March and April because of his activities in Westminster, and because, not surprisingly, he was not chosen by Parliament as a commissioner. William Rainborough was present at these meetings and so were two captains of Thomas's regiment, future officer-agitators, one of them a particular friend of the Colonel's. No progress was made towards peace between the Army and Parliament, partly because the chosen commissioners included exactly those Presbyterians whom the soldiers could least trust, and partly because, in any event, certain soldiers had taken matters into their own hands.[36]

The Army had taken the initiative from Westminster and devised its own plan for achieving a just settlement. Eight cavalry regiments within riding distance of headquarters had appointed 'agitators', or agents (the words are synonymous in the seventeenth century), to argue their case, first with the general officers and then with the rest of the world. They had their own cypher: 44 signified themselves the agitators, 55 the Army, 51 London, 92 may have been Joyce and 102, either Sexby or Chillenden.* Their agenda, dated 4th May, included the appointment of a council – the future General Council of the Army – with elected representatives, junior officers and men, as well as general officers at headquarters; provision for the preservation of unity, association with soldiers *and friends*† throughout the kingdom, redress of all arbitrary proceedings and an explanation of the need for reformation of civil government. The writer recognised the essential nature of communication and the need for 'able pen-men at Oxford and the Army where their presse be employed to satisfy and undeceive the people'. Once these aims had been realised, they confirmed that, with an Act of Indemnity, the Army could be reduced or disbanded.[37]

---

* In a later cypher, Colonel Rainborough was known as W.

† Italics mine. A parcel of copies of the Leveller March Petition was sent to the agitators within a fortnight of this letter being written. Poyntz' army in the north was also clearly referred to.

Soldier radicals in May 1647 showed an excellent grasp of essentials. The key figure in the political scene at that time was the King. Scarcely anybody in England was republican; a settlement without him was inconceivable. To leave him in the hands of an unrepresentative and untrustworthy Parliament, or Presbyterian officers loyal to that Parliament, would have been madness. It would also have been madness to allow the removal of the train of artillery in Oxford and all the ordnance and ammunition there to the Tower, as had been ordered. Colonel Rainborough's regiment was quartered between Petersfield and Portsmouth, waiting to embark for Jersey. The agitators were in touch with this regiment as early as 17th May and in accordance with instructions from them, it set off, mutinously, for Oxford some days later. The Commons heard of this on 28th May and ordered Colonel Rainborough to repair to his regiment immediately and restore order.

A letter from Rainborough to the House, written from Culham, three miles or so from Abingdon, was read on 2nd June and the Commons heard of the difficult and dangerous temper of the men, how crowded their quarters were and how impossible it was for the local people to provide them with food. The letter ends: 'I hope that the course I have taken ... will prevent any further miscarriage in them [the soldiers] ... although I cannot engage for them, yet there is nothing of care and duty wanting in him who is, Sir, Your most humble and faithful servant, Thomas Rainborough.'

This is a strange letter. It gives no information about the actual situation in Oxford or the recent activities of the regiment. In fact Rainborough's men had successfully seized £3,500 intended for paying off Colonel Ingoldsby's regiment and the two regiments together were guarding the guns in Oxford. An agitator, cypher 102, had written to other agitators on 28th May, telling them, among other things, of 1,000 horse who were to gather very secretly. (This may well be Cornet Joyce's force.) The writer explained: 'Colonel Rainborough is to go to his regiment, and it is by Oxford.' He added 'Let two horsemen go presently to Colonel Rainborough to Oxford and be very careful you be not over-witted'.[38]

Years later, Denzil Holles wrote that Colonel Rainborough had deliberately stayed in London throughout May 'pretending to prepare for that employment entrusted to him, in truth intending to give his soldiers a chance to mutiny'. Holles added that Rainborough had heard of his regiment's movements and kept the news to himself several hours before this was known in the House. Holles is a hostile witness and not necessarily in possession of the facts but communication between Thomas Rainborough and the agitators at this time is more than likely. He could have heard of all that had passed at the meetings at headquarters from his brother and from the representatives of his own regiment. He would have heard about his brother's stand against his Presbyterian colonel, Sheffield's, untruthful description of his own regiment's feelings in May. He would have been well aware of feeling in the army. Equally, the agitators would have had reason to believe that Thomas Rainborough might be sympathetic to them and their cause. It may be relevant that the earliest agitator letter referring to Rainborough's regiment immediately goes on to say 'send two more to London [where the colonel then was] to convey news'. As a siege expert he would have recognised the value and importance of the guns in Oxford.[39]

'Oxford, where our magazine is, we have well secured. I wish things at Holmby were as secure.' The agitator plans to secure the guns and money at Oxford and the person of the King at Holmby were linked. Cornet Joyce arrived at Holmby on 2nd June and left with the King in the direction of Newmarket on 4th June. Cromwell left Westminster at the same time and arrived at Newmarket, Fairfax's current headquarters and the designated rendezvous for the Army, that evening. The King was taken to Huntingdon: clearly, there were fears among the Army Grandees about bringing him too near the rendezvous. The Grandees claimed that Joyce had acted on his own authority. Charles I had more sense than to believe this. He said he would not accept the explanation if Joyce were not hanged. In September, the Cornet's promotion to the rank of captain was urged by Ireton and Rainborough.[40]

At Kentford Heath, outside Newmarket, a *Solemn Engagement* of the Army was drawn up to the effect that the soldiers would 'cheerfully and willingly disband ... or engage in further services either in England or Ireland' once their grievances had been satisfied. Without such satisfaction they would not willingly disband nor would they allow themselves to be divided. 'An unusual but ... necessary way ... of agreement among themselves' was for affairs to be placed in the hands of representatives of each regiment in the New Model to act in concert with the general officers as the General Council of the Army. Ireton, if, as seems probable, it was he who drew this *Engagement* up, ensured that officers predominated. All those of field rank – that is, majors and above – could sit and join in the debate if they wished; elected soldier-agitators for each regiment were to be balanced by officer-agitators selected from the junior ranks. A contemporary woodcut of the General Council of the Army in session shows the officers seated with their hats on, the agitators standing and bare-headed.[41] (See Fig. 6)

Colonel Rainborough and his regiment were present at the next rendezvous, which took place at Triploe Heath outside Cambridge on 10th June. It was necessary for the Army to be constantly on the move to avoid excessively burdening local populations and it was moving steadily and purposefully closer to London, the seat of power. A formal letter was sent from Royston to the City explaining the advance and attempting to allay the fears of the Londoners, confirming the safety of the City's wealth from 'poor, hungry soldiers'. This letter repeated the old claim that soldiers were Englishmen, desirous of the peace of the kingdom as much as satisfaction of their demands as soldiers:

We have said before, and profess it now, we desire no alteration of the Civil Government ... nor do we seek to open a way to licentious liberty under pretence of obtaining ease for tender consciences... Only we could wish that every good citizen, and every man that walks peaceably in a blameless conversation ... may have liberty and encouragement; it being according to the just policy of all States, even to justice itself.

Unfortunately, these two sentences were incompatible in the circumstances. The signatories to the letter, thirteen senior officers including Cromwell, Ireton and Rainborough, were to reveal themselves shortly as having different priorities.[42]

Tension was mounting throughout July in the Army and in the capital. One of the leading soldier-agitators endearingly described himself and his fellows at this time as 'but young statesmen'. His comment could be applied to many of the officers as well as the men. Colonel Rainborough was grappling with the complexities of the political situation himself. He supported Cromwell's suggestion that possible Army plans should be considered by a committee, including both of them, ten other officers and six agitators, before action was agreed, but his own distrust of talk and preference for action is summed up in the gloomy comment: 'For my part, I shall be weary of the meeting.'[43]

The action in question was a march on London to secure the expulsion of the eleven leading Presbyterian MPs from the Commons, the freedom of Leveller prisoners, including John Lilburne and Richard Overton, and the payment of arrears. Cromwell himself maintained that the Army was not without friends in Parliament and nothing worthwhile was to be gained by force. The agitators opposed delay and expressed their fears of the Presbyterians in London, supported by the London Militia, in Presbyterian control since May 1647, a force comparable to the New Model in terms of numbers.[44]

In the long run, Charles I was proved over-confident when he claimed: 'You cannot be without me; you will fall to ruin if I do not sustain you'. In the summer of 1647 when he was in touch with three different bodies – the Scots, Parliament and the New Model Army – all apparently anxious to come to terms with him, he could have been forgiven for thinking so. It seemed that all he had to do was see who would offer the most attractive terms. The quarrel between Parliament and the Army was distinctly in his interest.[45]

Cromwell and Ireton sincerely wanted to get his approval of the *Heads of Proposals*, the settlement on which Ireton had been working throughout July, before marching on London. It is impressive that the Grandees were so cautious and unwilling to use force, to employ the Army politically. Of course this may be explained by unworthy social fears such as those expressed in the recent past by John Hotham, Governor of Hull, or currently by his cousin, the evil Henry Cholmley, who urged peace between Parliament and the Army lest 'Clubbs and Clouted Shooes ... be too hard for both'.* It is possible, though, to credit Cromwell and Ireton with conscience. Thomas Rainborough was less aware than these two of the undesirability of using force – also more sympathetic to the agitators in their fear and impatience. He was a Londoner, as were many of his regiment, and he may have had a more accurate idea about feeling in the capital than the Grandees. There was, in fact, a sharp difference between central and western parishes in the city, which were conservative and Presbyterian, and the eastern fringe, Southwark, Wapping and Tower Hamlets which, together with Westminster, were Independent, sectarian and Leveller.[46]

On 26th July, a Presbyterian mob of reformadoes (unemployed ex-soldiers) and apprentices besieged the Palace of Westminster and terrorised the Commons. In consequence the two Speakers, Lenthal and Manchester, together with fifty-seven Independent MPs and eight peers, left Westminster to seek refuge with the Army. This galvanised Fairfax, who mobilised the regiments encamped around Bedford and set off for London. Ireton, Rainborough, Hammond and Rich rode to Woburn and formally presented King Charles with the *Heads of Proposals*, the constitutional settlement drawn up by Ireton and agreed as a basis for discussion by the officers of the New Model, or by those of them who had seen it.

Thomas Rainborough had formed an opinion of Charles I

---

* See p. 67.

fifteen months earlier and 'of all the army seemed the least to wish accord [with him]'. He may not have been surprised but was certainly appalled by the arrogance with which the King refused the Army proposals. He stole away in the middle of the conference and posted to the Army at Bedford to tell them what had happened. He was followed by the courtier, Sir John Berkeley, who, according to his own account, told some of the agitators that the Colonel had got things wrong. The agitators doubtless knew whom to believe.[47]

On the night of 3rd–4th August, under the command of Colonel Rainborough, four regiments entered Southwark from the south side of the Thames. There was no resistance and many of the inhabitants actually welcomed the soldiers. The City itself was occupied without a blow or a shot. Discipline was excellent: 'T'was not heard of so much as an apple taken by any of them' – to the great admiration of all who beheld the 'poor, hungry soldiers' and to the relief of all property owners.[48]

In August Thomas Rainborough went to live in his brother's house in Fulham, conveniently placed between Westminster and Putney, where General Fairfax set up his headquarters and where meetings of the General Council were held, generally in the parish church. Within easy reach by river were the agitators, quartered at Hammersmith. The King was lodged in comfort and state at Hampton Court and regularly visited by Cromwell, Ireton and their wives – not by Colonel and Mrs Rainborough though.[49]

Relations between Rainborough and Cromwell in the late summer of 1647 were poor. Sir Lewis Dyve, a Royalist prisoner in the Tower who had made friends with his fellow-prisoner, John Lilburne, and therefore managed to hear news of the radicals, wrote gleefully to the King in early September. Potential divisions in the Army would be most welcome to him. Dyve explained that 'the faction in the army' (clearly those represented by the agitators) might get a leader to balance Cromwell whose reputation was in decline with the common soldiers. Rainborough's credit with the soldiers was described as 'not inferior to any officer in the army'. He said that Rainborough was a man who would act in accordance with his own principles rather than another man's – a bit of information which can scarcely have been news to the King who had so recently met him. John Evelyn later described Dyve as 'a valiant gentleman but not a little given to romance when he spake of himself'. Nevertheless he is reliable on other matters and was well-informed about contemporary events in London. Lilburne was not his only source.[50]

Cromwell was increasingly suspected by the Levellers and also the soldiers for his association with the King and determination to come to terms with him. A lying rumour had been going round to the effect that he was to be made Earl of Essex and captain of the King's Guard in exchange for services rendered. Even Hugh Peter at this time accused Cromwell of being too much the courtier and Cromwell himself later admitted that he had been 'dazzled'. At the regular Thursday meeting of the General Council on 16th September in discussing a resolution to press Parliament to treat with the King on the basis of the *Heads of Proposals* matters between Rainborough and Cromwell reached a climax. Rainborough told Cromwell roundly: 'One of us must not live'.[51]

Thomas Rainborough's fury with the Lieutenant-General may be explained not only by a difference of opinion over Charles I but also by an incident which took place earlier the same day during a meeting of the Committee for the Admiralty. The subject under discussion then was the appointment of a Vice-Admiral to succeed William Batten, a dangerous and treacherous man so far as the Independents were concerned. He had been involved in the escape by sea of five of the Army's most hated Presbyterian MPs in August and was secretly involved in negotiations with the Scots, planning to hand the navy over to them. His chaplain, Samuel Kem, was a crypto-Royalist. The alignment of Royalists, Presbyterians and Scots was most dangerous to Independents and, of course, radicals, and it was highly desirable that the navy should be placed in trustworthy hands. The navy was not politically conscious in the way the Army had become and had not responded to the agitators' overtures in the summer. It had to be 'new-modelled' before it would accept Cromwellian officers in the Commonwealth period. So far as religion was concerned, the sailors were strictly Presbyterian, in all other respects, as Clarendon described them: 'a nation by themselves'. For the Independents Thomas Rainborough was an obvious choice as Vice-Admiral, politically, and because of his sea-going experience. His appointment was, however, opposed by Cromwell in an underhand fashion.[52]

Cromwell preferred Richard Deane for the post. Deane had had a much less distinguished military career than Rainborough to date but, like Rainborough, he did have the advantage of experience at sea. He had served under Thomas Rainborough's father, and the Colonel was a witness at his wedding in May 1647. It was doubtless through this family connection that Rainborough heard of Cromwell's scheme to keep him out while appearing to remain on strictly friendly terms. It had been decided by Cromwell and his 'Cabinet Council' that Northumberland should put forward Deane's name at the Committee for the Admiralty while Cromwell pretended to support Rainborough. The post would then go to Deane. At the crucial meeting, a furious quarrel was heard from behind closed doors by Captain Creamer in Rainborough's regiment, who then reported it to Lilburne. At this stage Cromwell capitulated and eleven days later the Commons approved Colonel Rainborough's appointment as Vice-Admiral of the Fleet for the next Winter Guard and agreed to pay him £1,000 as part of 'the arrears due to him for his service to Parliament'.

Various motives have been suggested for Cromwell's behaviour. He may have thought Rainborough too dangerous on account of his politics to be trusted with power at sea. He may have been so aware of feeling in the navy as to realise that Rainborough would never make a success of the job – though this would not explain the underhand nature of his dealing. Peace between the two men was, in fact, restored on 16th September but not political agreement. Six days later, in the Commons, Henry Marten proposed a Vote of No Further

Addresses to the King, with Thomas Rainborough as one of the tellers; Oliver Cromwell was teller for the other (successful) side.

Thomas Rainborough's regiment was subsequently given to Richard Deane and it has been suggested that Rainborough himself came to the debates at Putney, without any formal right to be there, to protest about this and his own consequent loss of pay. Of course Fairfax and Cromwell continued to draw pay as colonels of horse and foot regiments when acting as generals; this was normal. When Richard Deane was appointed 'General at Sea' in 1649, he retained command of the regiment, as did other 'Generals at Sea' like Blake. In September 1647 Thomas Rainborough was meanly treated. Honourable debate between him and the others at Putney is the more impressive.[53]

The civilian radicals were becoming increasingly impatient in the autumn of 1647. They distrusted the Grandees* – with reason – and the agitators – with less reason. They remained convinced of the desirability of associating with the Army and, to this end, successfully organised the appointment of new agents in five cavalry regiments.† Thomas Rainborough's relations with these new agents are difficult to determine. Dyve says that he was suspect with them because the House of Commons had voted him £1,000 of his arrears and confirmed his appointment as Vice-Admiral. Anything the Commons approved was anathema to the Levellers. On the other hand, Robert Huntingdon, a major in Cromwell's regiment who quarrelled with Cromwell in 1648, alleged that the Lieutenant-General had urged the 'outing' of Rainborough and Marten from the House and the Army because they were involved with the new agents in preparing 'several printed papers' and inciting the Army to mutiny. Colonel Rainborough apparently met 'Buff-Coat', Robert Everard, one of the new agents, for the first time at Putney but he said that he had seen 'this paper', the *Agreement*, by chance, before the debates began.[54]

---

*A pejorative term for Army leaders.

†Other regiments, foot as well as horse, followed suit.

The 'several printed papers' referred to by Huntingdon were the outcome of discussions which took place in September and October between the new agents and the civilian Levellers, John Wildman and Maximilian Petty. A long paper was prepared and handed to General Fairfax on 18th October. The Army's old grievances are listed in detail, together with their embarrassment at burdening their fellow-countrymen with the expense of free quarter and their dislike of the official attitude that as soldiers they existed only to serve the State and had forfeited their rights as free men. The solution was for the Army and the people to associate for all their rights and freedoms as soldiers and commoners. A 'law paramount', or written constitution, was proposed whereby Parliament should be elected every two years by all the free-born of twenty-one and upwards, excluding delinquents, this Parliament not to be adjournable or dissolvable by the King or by any other authority than itself. Suggestions were made about taxation, the plight of prisoners and the need to simplify the law.[55]*

The 'law paramount' was condensed and simplified into a much more sophisticated document, shorn of material relevant only to the immediate circumstances of 1647, entitled *An Agreement of the People*. In the *Agreement*, four proposals were made: that there should be a redistribution of seats, dissolution of the present Parliament, biennial elections in future and sovereignty of Parliament – with the electors reserving the fundamental rights of freedom of conscience and equality before the law and condemning pressing of troops and retrospective judgements. This was ready for discussion at the meeting of the General Council of the Army on 28th October, making it a vitally important one, very fully attended and reported verbatim, so far as he was able to keep up with the speakers, by William Clarke, one of the assistants to John Rushworth, secretary to Fairfax and the Council of War.[56]

The chairman of the most famous debates in British military history only enjoyed a courtesy title in the Army at the

---

* It has been suggested that Edward Sexby was the principal author of the *Case of the Army*.

time. Cromwell's commission had lapsed in July 1646; he took the chair because Fairfax was unwell. John Lilburne later concluded that now he was 'but a Usurper in the Army ... not King Oliver but Mr Oliver.'[57] No technical weakness of title, however, could affect Cromwell's standing in the New Model. Thomas Rainborough also had considerable standing among the soldiers but no official right to be present. He had been deprived of his regiment but fortunately had not yet gone to sea. Cromwell had the grace – or the political sense – to welcome him at Putney. Although Rainborough had no position in the Army in November 1647 and therefore no right to attend meetings of the General Council, he was regularly appointed to its committees up until 8th November, when Cromwell dismissed the agitators, an essential element in the General Council, back to their own regiments. This is a measure of the influence which the Colonel wielded.

On the first day of the debates, Cromwell and Ireton had to defend themselves against the charge of subservience both to the King and to Parliament. (In the Commons only eight days previously, Cromwell had made a long and impassioned speech in defence of monarchy.) Ireton was determined to put the civilian, John Wildman, in his place by reverting to a discussion of the Army's *Engagement* (or contract) of 5th June, drafted by himself, not to disband or divide without satisfaction for their grievances. He wanted, in fact, to put the clock back by four months. Cromwell expressed anxiety about the *Agreement* in front of him. There was no reason, he said, to suppose that another paper, equally plausible, might not be produced in the future. Neither Cromwell nor Ireton had the courage at this point to contemplate a radical political settlement. Thomas Rainborough's first speech on that first day showed his ability to face facts, put the *Engagement* of 5th June in its context and accept the *Agreement* as a basis for discussion. He expressed the hope that the Army would not divide and he admitted the difficulties of the present situation.

Truly, I think the Parliament were very indiscreet to contest with the King if they did not consider first that they

43

should go through difficulties: and I think there was no man that entered into this war, that did not engage to go through difficulties. And I shall humbly offer unto you ... that truly I think, let the difficulties be round about you – have death before you, the sea on each side of you and behind you – and are you convinced that the thing is just, I think you are bound in conscience to carry it on; and I think at the last day it can never be answered to God, that you did not do it. For I think it is a poor service to God and the kingdom, to take their pay and decline the work.[58]

Rainborough also pointed out that 'the just and equitable laws that the people of England are born to' actually represent past 'scufflings' and entrenchments on the once-enjoyed privileges of their rulers. He acknowledged the need for two or three days' discussion of the current proposals which neither he nor Everard nor Petty saw as a definitive statement of a final settlement. He supported the suggestion of one of the Anabaptist officers that time should first be spared for a prayer-meeting – a suggestion which Cromwell also endorsed. The prayer-meeting was fixed for the morning of the next day, Friday 29th October, to be held in Ireton's brother's house, and to be followed by a return to business in the afternoon.*

In fact Thomas Rainborough did not attend the prayer-meeting. At the afternoon session he apologised for his absence, explaining that ill-health had compelled him to go to London on the previous evening. It seems probable that what he was really doing was conferring with civilian radicals there, those who had drawn up the *Agreement* with the help of the new agents. He virtually admitted this himself when, later in the afternoon of 29th October, he urged speed and an end to debating irrelevancies such as previous engagements. He said

---

* Ireton himself had urged that the prayer-meeting should be held in a house rather than a church. This is consistent with Puritan extreme distrust of outward forms. Churches were sometimes described by them as 'steeple houses'. Just as the Council could meet regularly in a church to discuss secular business, so God could be 'publicly sought' in a private house.

he had good private authority for 'going the quickest way to work': debating the *Agreement*. Cromwell had wished this paper to be considered first by a committee of twelve officers, six Agitators, two civilians, Wildman and Petty, and representatives of the new agents. Rainborough emphasised the urgency of the matter and the desirability of debating with as many people present as possible. The high quality of the ensuing debate is the more impressive in view of the fact that the previous day's debate had lasted far into the evening and the present discussion carried on immediately from an intense and lengthy session of prayer – or, in the Colonel's case, from a hasty ride from Putney to the centre of London and back – as well as a probable series of talks.[59]

The *Agreement* was read and the first article repeated: 'That the People of England being at this day very unequally distributed ... for the election of their Deputies in Parliament, ought to be more indifferently proportioned, according to the number of the Inhabitants...' Ireton asked whether 'the people of England' meant everyone or the original electors, 40-shilling freeholders in the counties and a varied franchise in the boroughs. Battle was joined between him and Rainborough.[60]

Ireton said that he was in favour of equal distribution of seats but not an extension of the franchise. His reason for saying this was that he 'would have an eye to property'. Property, for him, was sacred and inalienably connected with the right to vote. Cromwell supported him; men who owned no more than their breath, as he put it, their existence, in fact, should have no voice in elections. Rainborough's view can best be expressed in his own words:

> For really I think that the poorest he that is in England hath a life to live, as the greatest he; and therefore truly, sir, I think it's clear, that every man that is to live under a government ought first by his own consent to put himself under that government; and I do think that the poorest man in England is not at all bound in a strict sense to that government that he had not had a voice to put himself under.

45

This is plain enough. Rainborough finished his speech by questioning whether any Englishman could doubt this conclusion.

Ireton and Cromwell clearly could. They were amazed and horrified. Rainborough was charged with attacking property and encouraging anarchy. He denied these charges and explained that we all have the God-given gift of reason. God gave men reason in order that they might use it. This gift of reason without property, he said, may seem a small thing, but half a loaf is better than nothing if a man is hungry. Nothing in the Law of God or the Law of Nature or the Law of Nations justifies a propertied franchise though it is true that the Law of God specifically confirms the institution of property in the commandment: 'Thou shalt not steal'. When Ireton quoted Scripture to justify the established order: 'Honour thy Father and Mother', Rainborough showed himself no Bible fundamentalist. He distinguished between known fathers and mothers and imposed authority. If the people of England have no voice in choosing their 'Fathers and Mothers' they cannot be bound to obey them.[61]

Debate continued on the issue of the franchise. Ireton qualified his original statement: he said he was not opposed to extending the franchise but opposed to giving it to the property-less. Thomas Rainborough, supported by Edward Sexby, demanded to know what the soldiers, for the most part not men of property, had been fighting for. He said that he had nothing at all of what he fought for – in this instance clearly speaking in general terms and of what he wanted for others since he himself was a man of property, inherited from his father in 1642, and entitled to the pay of a vice-admiral. He apologised for speaking with passion but urged a vote in the General Council so that at least all those present would 'know each other's mind'. This suggestion was ignored, and after more abortive discussion of property in relation to the franchise and the problem of foreigners and servants, Rainborough suggested a rendezvous of the whole Army and settlement as had previously been promised in its printed engagements or contracts. He clearly hoped for general acceptance of the

Agreement by the whole Army, as had happened with the *Engagement* at Kentford Heath on 5th June.

Ireton quickly said that the engagement that the Army should not divide was not to be taken in a *physical* sense; there was no need for the whole Army to be assembled at one meeting. He feared that the soldiers would support the *Agreement* unanimously and vociferously, and this was exactly what he and Cromwell did not wish. Rainborough sarcastically pointed out that Ireton had an advantage when it came to interpreting the *Engagement* of 5th June since he had drawn it up. No pre-contract could or should prevent men from dividing in their opinions.[62]

The debate on the franchise on 29th October showed a fundamental difference of opinion in principle between Rainborough and Ireton. Rainborough believed in the innate reasonableness and justice of individuals. He trusted (wrongly) that the united Army would support the constitution proposed by the Levellers, the *Agreement of the People*. Ireton had no belief in the natural rights of individuals and regarded the preservation of property as sacred. He maintained that property would be endangered by democracy. He claimed that soldiers had fought against royal absolutism and for the rule of law and the right to be governed by a representative body of 'those that had the interest of the kingdom', together with the freedom to make money and 'get estates'. He disliked the idea of a general rendezvous in case Rainborough's assessment of the temper of the soldiers was correct. He preferred the idea of smaller assemblies which could be more easily influenced or intimidated.

A committee which met on Saturday 30th and Sunday 31st October was appointed to consider the franchise question, the Army papers (163 pages, collected and printed in September 1647, brandished by Cromwell on the first day of the debates but much too long and involved to be used then) and the *Agreement*. This committee of eighteen men, including both the Rainboroughs and Sexby as well as Cromwell and Ireton, produced its report on 4th November, impressively practical and showing that men of widely differing opinions had

47

achieved compromise. It was agreed that the vote should be given to all who were not servants or beggars and specifically to all of Parliament's soldiers ... although they have not 40 shillings a year in freehold land.[63]*

Rainborough had taken time off from this committee on Sunday 31st to visit John Lilburne in the Tower, the first meeting between these two men who would have known each other well by reputation and who had served in the same theatre of the war in 1644. Dyve reported to the King that the two had conferred for two hours and that Rainborough was the likeliest man to become head of the faction in the Army which intended to purge Parliament and secure those officers who were their enemies. According to Dyve, this faction intended no harm to the King, and Rainborough himself 'proclaimed good sentiments to him'. Charles I was sceptical, urging caution where Rainborough was concerned, and Dyve's next report admitted that he could not be sure whether Rainborough's words, repeated to himself by Lilburne and 'some others who were present', were to be taken literally or not. Thomas Rainborough knew Charles I well enough to form an accurate assessment of his character. The King had applied to him personally in June 1646 for a safe conduct to London and received short shrift. He had heard with his own ears the arrogance with which the King refused the Army proposals in July 1646. One of his Putney speeches explained that, unlike Ireton, or unlike a view expressed by Ireton in the recent past, he did *very much care* whether there be a king or no king, lords or no lords, property or no property...' He may well have been opposed to Charles I without being anti-monarchy. At the General Council meeting on 5th November he successfully pressed for the sending of a letter to the Commons from

---

* Manhood suffrage, implied in Rainborough's reference to 'the poorest he in England', without secret ballot would have actually *increased* the power of employers and landlords at the expense of the rest. The committee therefore came to the conclusion that servants and beggars (i.e. those in receipt of alms) should be denied the vote. There is no reason to suppose, in fact, that reform of the franchise in the seventeenth century would not have been followed by secret ballot as it was in the nineteenth century – a prelude to manhood suffrage achieved in stages.

the Council, signed by William Clarke, denying any support in the Army for the current approach to the King by Parliament which Cromwell had returned to Westminster to champion on that same day. Ireton was so angry about this letter that he stormed out of the meeting and Fairfax, who was in the chair having recovered from the illness which had kept him from the earlier debates, obviously disliked it. He neither signed the letter personally nor sent an accompanying note with it to the Speaker, which was his usual practice. For the moment it looked as if the radicals in the Army might triumph.[64]

Cromwell and Ireton acted with great sense and sound instinct when faced, at this point, by virtual defeat at Putney. All news of the continuing debates was blacked. The transcript of proceedings for 5th November was destroyed by their order. The agitators were sent back to their regiments and a committee was appointed to decide what should be put before the soldiers at the three planned rendezvous. This committee of eighteen men included William Rainborough and the soldier-agitators Allen and Lockyer, but was dominated by Cromwell and Ireton and their supporters. It produced a paper which dealt exclusively with Army matters and outlined Fairfax's conditions for carrying on as General. Not surprisingly, these included the demand that 'everyone should be obedient to the General, the Council of War, and each to his superior officer'. Fairfax, whose reputation in the Army was untarnished and whose standing was unquestioned, would rendezvous the Army in person.[65]

The news of the King's escape from Hampton Court was heard on Friday 12th November. He had escaped, so it was said, because he feared a Leveller plot to murder him, and his escape from gaol was eased by his gaoler, Colonel Whalley, one of Cromwell's cousins. By 15th November it was known that he had arrived at the Isle of Wight, where the governor was another of Cromwell's cousins, Colonel Hammond. It is most unlikely, in spite of contemporary suspicions, that Cromwell had planned or instigated the escape. It was, however, very lucky for him because it renewed fear in the Army of the consequences of division and emphasised the need for loyalty and obedience to their old officers.

Thomas Rainborough was well aware of the danger inherent in the situation and full of suspicion of Cromwell and Ireton. When the news broke in the Commons, on receipt of a letter from Cromwell himself, he asked whether the King might not still be secreted in some part of Hampton Court, 'it being a great house, and there ready to act some great designe.' He went on to tell the House what danger was to be expected from the rendezvous. He clearly suspected that Cromwell and Ireton might produce the King in front of the soldiers. (How dangerous this would have been was subsequently demonstrated when the obedient soldiers shouted: 'For the King and Sir Thomas' at Ware.) The House debated deferring the rendezvous but could not do so because the regiments involved were already on the march. Rainborough was one of the Commons committee appointed on 12th November to look into Charles I's escape.[66]

On 15th November Rainborough attended the rendezvous at Corkbush Fields outside Ware which he had no right or authority to do. He presented Fairfax formally with a copy of the *Agreement* and a petition justifying the soldiers' action and saying that there seemed no hope that their native rights or the foundations of freedom would be secured but by this agreement, which now carried the slogan: 'England's Freedom, Soldiers' Rights' written on its back.

Many copies of this document had been circulated among the soldiers earlier in the day. With cool courage Fairfax reviewed the soldiers, regiment by regiment, and read, or had read to them, the paper drafted by the committee appointed of eighteen, a paper which dealt with the soldiers' grievances and left political matters to Parliament – a future Parliament, to be freely and equally elected in a manner which was not specified. Fairfax started with the mutinous regiment of Colonel Harrison, ordering the soldiers to remove from their hats copies of the *Agreement* with its accompanying slogan. Cromwell physically assisted Fairfax by trying to seize some of the papers himself. This regiment submitted easily, with the soldiers removing the offending *Agreement* themselves while Fairfax went on to review the seven regiments lawfully present.

The last regiment to be addressed, which arrived without orders in the afternoon of 15th November, gave the most trouble. It was drawn up in battle array under Captain-Lieutenant Bray, no other officers being present. The soldiers had the *Agreement* in their hats and had been in a state of mutiny since 23rd October when they had refused to march north as they had been ordered. Two soldiers had been killed and a junior officer had lost his hand. At Ware they attacked an officer of a neighbouring regiment with stones. Cromwell and others rode among the soldiers to restore order and destroy copies of the *Agreement*. Eight soldiers were court-martialled, found guilty and sentenced to death. All but three were pardoned; these three cast lots for their lives on the basis that the loser would be shot by the other two. Richard Arnold was shot at the head of the regiment and thus became the first Leveller martyr. Captain Bray was condemned to be court-martialled by the Council of War as were two other officers illegally present at the rendezvous. An officer who was also a recruiter MP was sent to Westminster under escort to be disciplined. The same fate probably overtook Thomas Rainborough, and both Houses ordered that he should not go to sea until the business had been examined, the Commons by a majority of only three, showing what personal support he still had there.[67]

The failed mutiny at Corkbush Field, followed by the two orderly rendezvous at St Albans and Kingston, was a blow to Thomas Rainborough and to the civilian radicals. John Lilburne, currently allowed out from the Tower by day without a keeper, and Richard Overton, who had been waiting hopefully in Ware for news, returned to London 'sick at heart'. Twenty thousand Spitalfields weavers whose support had been canvassed had not attended the rendezvous. Neither Edward Sexby, soldier-agitator of Fairfax's regiment of horse and therefore entitled to be present, nor William Rainborough, whose regiment attended mutinously without its officers, gave

51

any assistance to Thomas Rainborough on the day, and his own conduct seems to have been hesitant. He proffered the *Agreement* and petition to Fairfax tentatively and was easily waved aside. Quite probably he realised how hopeless the situation was when he saw that only two regiments, eighteen hundred men, were there against orders, as opposed to the dutiful seven, about six thousand men. He must also have sadly noticed the lack of civilian supporters. A Royalist newsletter from London, dated 15th November and therefore written before the writer could have known what actually happened, said: '[Colonel Rainborough] doth conceive his party will prove too weak at this meeting.'[68]

The planning of the Ware mutiny had been inadequate but there had been very little time and the escape of the King had shocked all. Many soldiers realised that they might soon find themselves in the field again and this thought would drive political considerations from their minds. Others trusted the King still, as their cry 'the King and Sir Thomas' demonstrated. William Rainborough had been in much closer touch with the men of his regiment in recent months than Thomas was with any of the rank-and-file. He would have known how near the provisions in Fairfax's *Remonstrance*,* which he had helped to draft, came to calming the soldiers' most immediate fears. Mutiny is a very serious business, as its punishment shows, and not to be undertaken lightly. The split between religious and political radicals, so astonishing and embittering to the latter, had already begun to manifest itself in the autumn of 1647 and this had its own effect on the political attitude of the soldiers. Once the Saints† had turned their backs on the possibility of building Jerusalem here and now in England's green and pleasant land and ceased to preach accordingly, the soldiers lost the stimulus of sermons with an immediate and practical application. Political questions which had always been difficult for them to comprehend might be deferred in view of more fighting.[69]

---

*The paper read aloud to the soldiers on Corkbush Field, based on the *Desires of the Army* produced by the committee of eighteen.

† See p. 74.

For another month the King negotiated with the Grandees on the basis of their proposed constitution, the *Heads of Proposals*. He also continued to negotiate a fundamentally different deal with the Scots. He signed an *Engagement* with the latter on 26th December, agreeing to a three-year trial period for Presbyterianism in England, suppression of the Independents and the Sects, and the restoration of the King's power, including the royal veto and control of the armed forces. A second civil war was now inevitable. Thomas Rainborough's estimate of the King as a character who could not be trusted was proved correct and Cromwell acknowledged that he had been 'dazzled' by Charles I. At the meeting of the Army Council on 21st December Rainborough had apologised for his indiscipline, repudiating none of his political views. This formal apology saved Cromwell's face. He was able to give assurance to the Commons that Rainborough would be 'conformable' to the direction of himself and Ireton for the management of the whole business at sea. On 3rd January Cromwell spoke in the Commons, describing the King as a 'great dissembler', and the House voted by a majority of forty-nine to have no more dealings with Charles I. Three months earlier Cromwell had spoken passionately and at length in favour of a personal treaty with the King and acted as teller for the Ayes in a vote to this effect. Thomas Rainborough had been a teller for the Noes on that same occasion.[70]

Defence of the Isle of Wight was recognised as a priority once the King's dealings with the Scots were known, and the Commons ordered Rainborough to take up his command in the Solent without waiting for confirmation from the Lords. He did this with some style, arriving at Deal, the official residence of the Vice-Admiral, in a coach and four with an escort of trumpeters and soldiers and, as it turned out, with the cards stacked against him. In the first place, discipline in the navy had suffered during the long delay between Batten's dismissal and Rainborough's appointment in September 1647, and January 1648 when the latter was allowed to take up his appointment. Secondly there was an active Presbyterian group in the navy, supporters of Batten, inspired and encouraged by his agent and ex-chaplain, Samuel Kem, fundamentally opposed to Rainborough's politics and religion. Lastly, the county of Kent, always more in sympathy with the King than with Parliament but isolated from other Royalist areas and unable to escape from Parliament's control between 1642 and 1647, was at last able to manifest its Royalist and Anglican leanings. Most of Rainborough's seamen were natives of Kent and there was constant traffic between the mainland and the men afloat in the Downs.[71]

Rainborough was quickly aware of the dangers of a Royalist revolt. He urged the Commons to hurry up with sending out ships for the Summer Guard and appointing professionally competent, politically reliable commanders. Politically reliable did not necessarily mean the same thing to the Admiralty Commissioners, the Commons and the Lords. Disputes between the two latter over the appointment of commanders continued throughout March. The Earl of Warwick, whose reputation in the fleet remained high after he had been forced to resign as Lord High Admiral in 1645 as a result of the Self-Denying Ordinance, was a constant opponent of Rainborough's and influenced his fellow-members in the Lords.* He was patron of the treacherous Batten who remained a naval commissioner while actively plotting with Royalist agents in London. Samuel Kem worked steadily on his behalf from his vantage point as minister at Deal. Rainborough reminded the Commons of their promise to remove the parson to some other living but his plea went unheeded.[72]

The Commons' vote to the effect that Rainborough be ordered forthwith to sea took place on Christmas Eve. Christmas Day produced a riot in Canterbury, one of the most populous and prosperous cities in England, only sixteen miles, as the crow flies, from Deal. Parliament's order that Christmas should not be celebrated as a holiday and Holy day was disregarded.

---

* The House of Lords at this time numbered seventeen including the Speaker. By no means all members attended every session.

A congregation gathered at St Andrew's Church in the High Street to hear Divine Service and a Christmas sermon on Saturday 25th, rivalled by a 'mob of new saints' who tried to drown the preacher by making a commotion outside. Serious disorder resulted and a foot regiment had to be sent down in January. About forty of the rebels were imprisoned in Leeds Castle to await trial by due process of the law at the assizes in May. They were acquitted by a local jury, as might have been expected, and a petition was drawn up demanding a treaty between the King and both Houses, the disbandment of the Army, the Commonwealth to be governed by its known laws and no other, the Excise to be abolished and property to be preserved. A mass meeting at Blackheath was planned for 30th May, when the petition with all its signatures was to be presented.[73]

Rainborough wrote to the Committee of the Admiralty explaining that support for the King in the county of Kent was the chief cause of disturbance among the seamen. The naval mutiny in support of the King had, in fact, been carefully planned for some months but broke out precipitately in May as the result of a curious and, actually, unrelated incident. William Batten, designed to be the new Admiral, had been regularly meeting Royalist agents at the Hoop tavern in Leadenhall Street. Lucy, Countess of Carlisle, a veteran intriguer, provided communication between Royalists in England, the Queen in France and the King in the Isle of Wight. Through Samuel Kem they were in touch with the boatswain and the boatswain's mate on board Rainborough's flagship, the *Constant Reformation*.[74]

On 19th May, a strange young man arrived at Deal, 'on foot, and in an old black ragged suit, without any Companions but Lice'. He was escorted to Sandwich by the boatswain's mate from the *Constant Reformation*, one of the Royalist plotters, and enthusiastically welcomed as the Prince of Wales, whom he claimed to be, by the men of the *Providence*. The sailors, who had recently been paid in full, provided him with money and he established himself at the Bell Inn with a group of supporters. Although his intelligence service had warned him that Prince Charles was likely to leave France, the Vice-Admiral was not deceived. He instructed the Sandwich magistrates to detain the boy and wrote to the Speaker for orders. Rainborough was ordered to send the impostor by sea to London to be examined by the Commons but, by the time that this letter was received, Sandwich was in the hands of the Royalists and Parliament's control in the surrounding area was on the point of collapse.* Although Batten's schemes were not yet mature, Samuel Kem could not miss the opportunity afforded by the incident of the pretended Prince of Wales. He was busily distributing copies of the county petition, drawn up in the wake of the assizes, in all the ships in the Downs and successfully got on board the *Constant Reformation* when the Vice-Admiral was ashore inspecting the defences of Deal Castle. The crew declared themselves for the King and the Gentlemen of Kent, those officers and men who did not agree being sent below decks. Thomas Rainborough who could see and hear the commotion on board his ship from the leads of the Castle, waved his sword at the rebels before setting off to restore order. The sailors refused to allow him on board. They confirmed that he had been 'a loving and Courteous Colonel to them' and should therefore suffer no damage in person or property from them. They could not spare a ship to take him, his wife, sister and sister-in-law from the Castle to London but a Dutch fly-boat was found to take them to safety for 6d. It is hard to imagine a mutiny in which the commander and his family were accorded such treatment. They could not have escaped by land or sea if they had not been permitted to do so. The differences between Rainborough and his sailors were essentially political rather than personal.[75]

This information comes from a Royalist contemporary, Matthew Carter, Quarter-Master General of the forces raised in Kent, who went on to accompany those forces to Colchester. It is flatly contradicted by a subsequent 'Reason' given for the seamen's action: 'the insufferable pride, ignorance and

---

*The impostor, whose real name was Cornelius Evans, escaped to the Isle of Thanet with the help of some of the seamen but was later arrested and stood trial in London. The Kentish Royalists made no further use of him.

insolency of Colonel Rainborough, the late Vice-Admiral, alienated the hearts of his seamen'. A *Declaration of the Navy* was drawn up on 28th May, beginning: 'We ... refuse to be under the command of Colonel Rainborough by reason we conceive him to be a man not well affected to the King, Parliament and the Kingdom; and do hereby declare unto you, that we have unanimously joined with the Kentish gentlemen in their just petition to the Parliament.' The provisions of the Kentish petition concerning the need to treat with the King, to disband the Army, to preserve the known laws of the land and the privileges of Parliament were next listed. Three weeks later three 'Reasons' were added to this document: one that recent commissions in the navy had been granted by Parliament in its own name without reference to the name of the King; two, that several land-men had been made sea-commanders; and three, the character-assassination of Thomas Rainborough, quoted above. The first of these 'Reasons' is a straightforward statement of the navy's Royalist sympathies. The second is specious; distinctions were only just beginning to be drawn between land and sea service.* The success of Cromwell's 'Generals at Sea' in the 1650s proves this point. The third 'Reason' does not square with either Carter's description of what happened on 27th May or the fact of the safe removal of the Rainboroughs and Mrs Stephen Winthrop and all their children from Deal to London.

The Presbyterian, Warwick, with immense seafaring experience, was immediately appointed Admiral in place of Rainborough but proved equally unable to control the mutinous sailors. They repeated their determination to ally with the Kentish gentlemen. In June nine ships (of which two subsequently returned) set off for Holland and the Prince of Wales under Batten. By August there were eighteen ships professing loyalty to him as against fourteen, obedient to Warwick, and nine from Portsmouth whose allegiance was doubtful. The seamen were, above all, 'a fraternity', unwilling to fight against each other and 'jealous of those to-morrow by whom

---

* See p. 13.

they are governed to-day'. Batten's popularity proved short-lived. It was rumoured in the autumn of 1648, at the time of his murder, that Rainborough might succeed Warwick once again.[76]

Just as the Roundheads were, albeit unwillingly, aggressors in the First Civil War, the Second Civil War was provoked by the King and his supporters. In 1648 Presbyterians were prepared to make common cause with Royalists; Independents were not prepared to make any concessions to radicals. The Commons arrested John Lilburne after a temporary period of liberty, two months in all, and John Wildman after a tip-off from a Presbyterian minister before a Leveller mass meeting planned for 23rd January at Dartford could take place. In April the officers at Windsor disciplined some 'in the Armie who are yet faithful to the People' who had agitated for the Leveller and Army programme. It was not the moment for division or discussion in the Army. A two-day prayer-meeting was interrupted by news of Royalist successes in Wales, and Cromwell was despatched there at once. Berwick and Carlisle were captured by the Royalists and a Scottish invasion was expected. Royalist feeling in the City of London was growing. News of the rising in Kent and the mutiny in the fleet thus confirmed the renewal of war, a war which was to be much more brutal and bloodthirsty than the first had been.[77]

The rising in Kent was promptly and efficiently suppressed by Fairfax but about four thousand Kentish Royalists escaped over the Thames into Essex and made a stand in the walled town of Colchester. It was not a suitable place for prolonged defence and the Royalists initially planned to stay there for one night only. When Fairfax caught them up on 13th June they were loth to try breaking out in open country without even hedgerows for shelter because the Roundheads were strong in cavalry. The port was blockaded by six ships which had remained loyal to Parliament. Fairfax was unwilling to try storming the town because the Royalists were greatly superior in numbers. The ensuing siege lasted eleven weeks in horrible conditions – aggravated by exceptionally wet weather and flooding. Tempers rose on both sides and operations were marked by savagery and brutality on the part of besiegers and besieged.[78]

Thomas Rainborough did not stay long in London after losing his command in the navy. The technical problems involved in a siege such as Colchester would have appealed to him, as would the opportunity of serving under Fairfax. He was already on the spot, possibly with a small company of men, when a regiment became available for him. This was the Tower Guard, or Tower regiment, newly formed for the protection of the fortress when Fairfax became Lieutenant of the Tower in August 1647. It was sent to help the General in Kent and both the colonel and the lieutenant-colonel were killed in the first few weeks of the siege of Colchester, shot with poisoned bullets, either 'chewed ... and rolled in sand' (an effective poison in the days before antiseptic) or 'boiled in Coprice' (sulphate of iron, used in dyeing cloth or making ink). Use of these bullets, the seventeenth-century equivalent to chemical weapons, was contrary to the rules of war and the Roundheads retaliated by killing prisoners: 'many of those prisoners we took yesterday are ... dead of those wounds they received, merely for using poisoned bullets, who otherwise had received fair quarter.'[79]

With his experience of siege warfare and customary energy, Thomas Rainborough got to work at once to complete the ring of forts constructed by the besiegers with 'Fort Rainborough' on the north side of the town. The besieged had established a sniper-cum-look-out in the bell-chamber of St Mary at the Wall, a church with a strong, square tower, sited at the highest point of the town. One newspaper gave the credit for shooting this man, by repute the Royalists' 'best cannoneer', to Colonel Rainborough. The feat was attributed variously in other newspapers.[80]

There is no doubt that the credit of leading a most important raid on 25th July belonged to Colonel Rainborough. He led the Tower Guards at night across the swollen river from their fort to storm the Middle Mill, the last mill in the town remaining in operation and capable of turning the stocks of corn into bread. Rainborough's men cut the sluice which fed the mill and then tried to fire it. Three were killed and others were wounded: the Royalists successfully put out the fire with their hats filled with water. Enough damage was done to ensure that the mill was out of action by 6th August. Fairfax reported: 'We can take Colchester any time but we are so likely to take it by starving, there is no reason to cast away our men by storm'.[81]

The situation in the town was fast becoming desperate. Dysentery broke out, the side of a small dog was worth six shillings and starving women were jestingly told by the Royalist commander to eat their own children. On 22nd August five hundred women were sent out of the town by the besieged. They set off hopefully towards Colonel Rainborough's quarters. In accordance with the General's orders, he turned them back, first by firing cannon and muskets over their heads and then by sending his soldiers to threaten them with stripping. Four were stripped, and the women turned back. The Royalists refused to let them in and they spent a night in no man's land before being allowed back to their own homes. This was not the only time during the siege of Colchester that women had thrown themselves on Fairfax's mercy. On at least two previous occasions, women and children had tried to come out of the town, but once the Roundheads had decided, in order to save the lives of their own men, to starve the enemy into submission, they could not allow any reduction in the number of mouths to be fed.[82]

The Royalist leaders held a Council of War and decided to escape or perish; their soldiers understandably mutinied. Only those with horses, and that meant very few, had a chance of escaping, if the commanders got their way. On 27th August, Colchester surrendered on Fairfax's terms and Colonel Rainborough was one of the commissioners who signed the articles of surrender. The following day, the Tower Guards, with one other regiment of foot, entered the town.[83]

Colchester surrendered on terms which were most carefully

defined: fair quarter for inferior soldiers and townsmen, mercy for the officers. 'Fair quarter' was explained as warm clothing and food fit for prisoners; 'mercy' carried no assurance of quarter – the Lord General was free to put some immediately to the sword, although he intended chiefly to surrender them to the mercy of Parliament. The six Royalist commanders, who included an Italian, Sir Bernard Gascoigne, were excepted from mercy. The three peers were handed over to civil justice; one escaped, one was banished and one was executed. The other three were judged to be soldiers of fortune and liable to the jurisdiction of Fairfax and his Council of War. A Council of War, presided over by Fairfax and attended by Ireton, Whalley and Rainborough, was held on 28th August, the day after Rainborough's regiment had entered the town. Sir Charles Lucas, Sir George Lisle and Sir Bernard Gascoigne were condemned to death. The sentence was carried out that evening and Lucas and Lisle were duly shot; Gascoigne was reprieved at the last moment.[84]

Shock and outrage prevailed at the shooting of these two men; 'a new, unheard of way of condemning men in our nation', as Carter said, although he admitted that the sentence was in accord with the terms of surrendering to mercy. After the Restoration, a stone was erected on the site of the shooting, dedicated to the two men, inscribed with the words: 'by the command of Sir Thomas Fairfax, in cold blood barbarously murdered', and Charles II himself refused Fairfax's request that this should be taken down. Two hundred and thirty-two years after the incident, mention was made of 'a belief to this day that grass does not grow on the spot of the shooting (which is a fact) because it actually refuses to do so.'*[85]

Both Lucas and Lisle had broken their parole and promise, given at the end of the First Civil War, respectively at Stow-on-the-Wold and Faringdon, not to take up arms against Parliament again. At the Council of War which condemned the

---

*The current obelisk is embedded in gravel so there is no possibility, at the moment, of proof.

two men, Colonel Whalley quoted a precedent for killing in cold blood: Royalists had hanged fourteen men, 'most of them clothiers', on the same tree after the garrison of Woodhouse in Wiltshire had submitted to mercy in 1644. Sir Charles Lucas was reminded that he had killed two men with his own hands when the Stinchcombe garrison surrendered on the promise of fair quarter in 1645. Fourteen others of that same garrison were hanged.[86]

Thomas Rainborough was present at the Council of War which condemned Lucas and Lisle. He seems also to have been present at the executions. Clarke's account, the only source for the discussion which took place immediately before the shooting, does not mention him at all but Carter describes him, together with Ireton and Whalley, as 'spectator as well as actor in this inhumane tragedy'. He clearly did not play a leading part either in condemning Lucas and Lisle or in justifying the execution after it had taken place. After his own murder, itself a blatant infringement of the rules of war, the Royalist press accused him of having done so and getting no more than his just deserts. *Mercurius Melancholicus* commented:

> Rainborough here interr'd doth lye,
> With his nine Furies, Treachery,
> Ambition, Lust, Rebellion's fire,
> Pride, the Insatiate desire
> Of Blood; as witnessed ere-while
> The deaths of Lucas and Lisle,
> Sedition, Schisme, and the worst
> Of all the nine, Contention curst
> Even from his birth, tread softly here
> Lest that his furious Ghost appeare.

A satirical poem or song, *Colonel Rainborough's Ghost*, which came out the same week, took up the same theme. In a supposed conversation between Rainborough and his murderers, he was told:

We to you will straighthway show
For Lucas and Lisle dye you must.

The Royalists deliberately fastened the blame for the deaths
of Sir Charles Lucas and Sir George Lisle on Rainborough to
distract attention from the evil circumstances of his own
murder. There is no evidence that he played a leading part in
the affair although he would, undoubtedly, have condemned
those whom he held responsible for the misery of the besieged
town, the extent of its destruction and the sickly and starving
condition of its inhabitants.[87]

Cromwell's victory at Preston and the fall of Colchester virtually brought the Second Civil War in England to an end.
Political considerations once more came to the fore. Even
before these victories, or news of them, could have reached
London, an unsigned pamphlet had stressed the danger of
going to war before those expected to fight and kill each other
could be certain what they were fighting for. Soldiers had been
deceived in the past by the King, by Parliament and by great
men in the City and Army, the writer claimed. He concluded
by saying: If you engage at all, do it by Lawfull Authority, let
your Cause be declared, and just also, and let it be for the good
of the whole Nation, without which you will not only hazard
being Slaves, but also contract upon yourselves ... the guilt
of Murtherers.'[88]

There is an echo here of the Putney question, posed by
Edward Sexby and Thomas Rainborough: have the soldiers
been fighting all this time for nothing? The position of the
King still seemed to be the key to any settlement. Republicans
were very few and far between. Even Henry Marten,
Rainborough's friend, who had been imprisoned for a short
time in 1643 for doubting whether one man was wise enough
to rule us all, thought now that it would be better to have the
King restored by negotiation rather than forced on the country by the Scots. After Preston, of course, this was not a danger and the Vote of No further Addresses to the King was

repealed. A Leveller petition which claimed to have 40,000 signatures denied the right of veto to the King and the Lords but, by implication, confirmed their right to exist. The Levellers naturally feared a personal treaty between the King and the Commons with its strong Presbyterian element and, in fact, the Commons began negotiations with Charles I one week after the publication of this petition. The King was allowed to move from Carisbrooke to Newport on parole for the purpose of the discussions. The recruiter MP Edmund Ludlow, who was a republican, had already been down to Colchester to warn Fairfax of what he saw as 'a design to betray the Cause'.[89]

After Ludlow's visit, when Rainborough and Ireton were both still at Colchester with Fairfax, a former lieutenant-colonel, John Jubbes, a speaker at Putney who had resigned his commission in April 1648 from disgust with the Grandees, arrived with detailed proposals for a settlement. He later claimed that these proposals were approved by 'Colonel Rainborough and the rest of the other Colonels', only 'sticking' when they were shown to Ireton. Jubbes advocated the restoration of the King after an admission of blood-guiltiness, with a guaranteed revenue but without a right of veto; biennial Parliaments, elected by 40-shilling freeholders or those with £50 pounds' worth of personal property; equality before the law and freedom of conscience.[90]

Jubbes's description of the reception of his scheme was written eight months after his visit to Colchester and seven months after Thomas Rainborough's death. It sheds fitful light on Rainborough's political views in the autumn of 1648 because Jubbes himself is not always trustworthy and because evidence concerning the Colonel's attitude to the King and the monarchy is conflicting. In the Commons and in the Army Council a year earlier he had been in the van of the movement for no more dealings with Charles I. It seems that he had distrusted the King, personally, since the approach at Woodstock in April 1646 and the arrogant behaviour of the latter at Hampton Court in August 1647. On the other hand, in November 1647, Dyve had said that Rainborough professed good sentiments to the King and repeated this statement when challenged.[91]

Two of the Colonel's speeches at Putney, one of them very badly transcribed, throw some light on his attitude. When Ireton speciously claimed that if he saw the hand of God in the destruction of kings, lords and all distinctions and degrees, he himself would quietly acquiesce in their abolition, Rainborough answered: 'I do very much care whether [there be] King or no King, lords or no lords, property or no property; and I think if we do not all take care, we shall all have none of these very shortly.' Three days later, when one of the agitators referred to the continuation of the monarchy and the Lords as a principal issue dividing the debaters at Putney, Rainborough defended himself from the charge that he was one of their opponents.[92]

There was no illogicality, in fact, in opposing Charles I personally while continuing to believe in the institution of monarchy. The possibility of deposing him in favour of one of his sons had been seriously canvassed. There is no inherent contradiction between constitutional monarchy and the liberty of the individual. Thomas Rainborough's views on the franchise, individual rights and what was owed to the soldiers were expressed in such a way at Putney as to leave no doubt about his feelings but he was not certain about forms of government. The fact that he was prepared to discuss limitations of the power of the King and the Lords indicates that he was not necessarily concerned to abolish them. In one of his Putney speeches he did refer to the deposition of Richard II: the removal of a despotic individual (by the undesirable means of murder) but not the abolition of monarchy itself. A monarch without the right of veto or control of the armed forces could scarcely endanger the safety of the people.

In September 1648 the Tower Guards, Colonel Rainborough's regiment, were ordered north by Fairfax to take part in the siege of Pontefract Castle, where the Royalists, with food for a twelvemonth and no hope of mercy, were prepared to make a prolonged and desperate stand. The Colonel himself was delayed in London organising a month's pay for his men, and arrived in Doncaster, twelve miles from Pontefract, on 14th October, four days after they had halted there to wait for him. He had recently survived an attack by three well-mounted Royalists on the road between London and St Albans. London was full of such incidents. In the same week, a major and a captain in the Army were killed and there was rumour of a plot to massacre eighty of the MPs who opposed the Newport treaty.[93]

Before the arrival of the Tower Guards and their colonel, the siege of Pontefract was being conducted in a most dilatory fashion by Sir Henry Cholmley, a local gentleman appointed by the County Committee. Besiegers and besieged fraternised, holding a cessation, parley and horsefair at which horses were sold to Cholmley's men to the accompaniment of toasts: 'Here is to thee, Brother Roundhead and I thank thee, Brother Cavalier.' The enemy, as Colonel Rainborough reported, ranged nightly over a ten-mile area, regularly returning to the castle with prisoners and booty. A letter from York confirmed: 'There is no difference amongst the Pontefract-Blades ... they agree too well.' The writer explained that the surrounding country was suffering and that it was to be hoped that Rainborough would be able to control the marauding Cavaliers.[94]

At the moment of his death Thomas Rainborough recognised that he had been betrayed. His last words were to this effect. Sir Henry Cholmley was the arch-traitor and he escaped unscathed. He and his elder brother were both members of the Long Parliament and fought on different sides in the First Civil War, remaining on excellent personal terms. The loyalty of both brothers was primarily reserved for their own county, Yorkshire, and for the existing social order. Sir Henry, therefore, accepted the job of commanding the siege of Pontefract when it was offered him by the County Committee and he was outraged by Fairfax's appointment of Rainborough as his superior. He would accept Cromwell in command, so he said, and the Committee wrote to Cromwell asking him to accept this.[95]

A letter of Cholmley's to the Speaker, dated 8th July 1647, shows how far he differed from Thomas Rainborough in terms of what the war was about and what the winners might hope to get from it. He explained then that Parliament had, he feared, more enemies than friends in Yorkshire, willingly looking for peace on any terms. The common soldiers, he reported, were 'so well agitated' by Lilburne that they were in the same case as the soldiers in the south. There could be no chance of co-operation between commanders whose views differed so radically. Cholmley finished his letter urging peace between Parliament and the Army for the peace of the kingdom, 'otherwise ... Clubbs and Clouted Shooes will in the end be too hard for them both.' He was not a man to care for the poorest he in England or to co-operate with Rainborough, champion of the latter.[96]

The day after he arrived in Doncaster on 14th October 1648, Rainborough wrote to Fairfax, rather a despairing letter outlining his difficulties with Sir Henry, unwilling, as he said, to acquaint the General with details of the jealousies involved but saying, uncharacteristically, that he would be glad to be excused the service. 'I can carry on', he went on to say, 'provided I have reinforcements of horse and ammunition.' He planned to wait in Doncaster for an answer to this letter, keeping two companies of his regiment in the town with him and billeting the others in the surrounding countryside in order to spread the load of feeding them. He thought that he himself was safe with a guard of sixty foot-soldiers since 'it was at least pretended', as *The Moderate* later reported grimly, that the Royalist stronghold was surrounded.[97]

Twenty-two men, led by Captain William Paulden, escaped easily from Pontefract on the night of 27th October and made their way by slow stages to Doncaster. They were able to take cover in the wooded neighbourhood of the river Cheswould, a tributary of the river Don, until sunrise on Sunday 29th (about 7.30 a.m.). A spy in the town was ready to tell them how it was guarded and where Colonel Rainborough was billeted. They presented themselves at St Sepulchre's Gate, south-west of Doncaster, after meeting the Royalist spy who had a Bible in his hand for identification purposes. The plan was for six of the party to fall on the backs of the guard at St Mary's Gate bridge, north of the town, and make good the retreat to Pontefract by the most direct route, six to fall on the main guard, six to patrol the streets and four to proceed to Colonel Rainborough's lodgings.[98]

All went as planned. The only person to offer resistance to this surprise attack was Thomas Rainborough himself. The men entered on the pretext of bringing letters from Cromwell which Rainborough was probably expecting. It seems likely that kidnapping rather than murder was intended and that the Royalist plan was to exchange Rainborough for Sir Marmaduke Langdale, a prisoner in Nottingham Castle who had, in fact, escaped on the previous day, unbeknown to Rainborough's attackers. Thomas Rainborough was disarmed, brought down from his chamber and urged to keep silent while he was forcibly put on a horse and led away. When he saw that there were only four men, albeit armed, against himself, his lieutenant and his sentinel, he put up a spirited resistance, seizing the sword of his captor while his lieutenant got hold of a pistol. They were overpowered, however, and both killed. A maid, the only witness, heard Rainborough's last cry that he had been betrayed, and the triumphant cry of the attackers; 'Farewell Rainborough. Farewell Cavaliers'.[99]

This strange cry has given rise to the speculation that Thomas Rainborough's murder was a plot planned by his own side who feared his politics and his following and thus devised his removal from the scene. It is true that the Governor of Pontefract Castle, Colonel Morris, sent a sealed letter to Sir Henry Cholmley, saying that he himself had now decided the controversy about the Roundhead command, and Cholmley is said to have laughed immoderately. Cholmley's complicity in the murder was rumoured in many contemporary reports, Royalist as well as Roundhead. He was never examined about the affair or reprimanded for his lax surrounding of the Castle which had enabled the Royalists to succeed. The raiding party, incidentally, returned to Pontefract in daylight and entered the Castle unmolested, in full view of the Cholmley horse.[100]

Five months later, in March 1649, John Lilburne attacked the Grandees in the Army for having deliberately sent Colonel Rainborough to 'dangerous and unhappy' service at Pontefract, regardless of the problem of divided authority and a commander appointed by the local committee. Lilburne confirmed that Rainborough's brother was given no help in searching after and prosecuting the causers of that 'bloody and inhumane Butchery'.[101]

The Commons had ordered Cromwell to make an official enquiry into Rainborough's murder in early November when the Lieutenant-General himself took over the siege, expecting a long one because of the practical difficulties which Rainborough had already noticed, and the fact that a desperate garrison was not likely to give up easily. When Cromwell went south in December 1648 to attend to political matters, Lambert succeeded him in command at Pontefract and, four months later, showed himself 'a merciful man to war criminals'. Even the Royalist press had admitted, at the time, that the killing of an unarmed man was contrary to the laws of war.[102]

When Pontefract surrendered in March 1649, six men were exempted from mercy: the Governor, Colonel Morris, Lieutenant Austwick and Cornet Blackburn, who had been on the raid which resulted in Rainborough's death, and three others. These six were given two days to escape if they could when the garrison surrendered. Morris and Blackburn got away but were captured ten days later and subsequently executed. One man was killed in the escape attempt and the other three, who included Austwick, the alleged killer of Rainborough, survived, having been successfully hidden by their fellows in the Castle. Captain William Paulden, who led the Doncaster raid, had died one month before the surrender. His brother Thomas, who had also been on the raid, escaped and wrote an account of the affair, published fifty-four years after it had happened.

In December 1648 when the House of Commons was

purged by the Army as a prelude to setting up the Commission to try the King, Henry Cholmley was secluded and returned to his Yorkshire estates. In 1660 he assisted his Yorkshire neighbours, including Fairfax, with plans for the Restoration. In 1662, presumably as a reward, he was given command of a regiment by General Monck. John Lilburne's complaint that William Rainborough had received no help or encouragement in searching out and punishing his brother's murderers thus contains more than a grain of truth. The Commons may have ordered an enquiry into the murder, recognised as such and contrary to the rules of war, but they did virtually nothing to prosecute either the enquiry or the criminals, Royalists and negligent Roundheads alike, either immediately or after the fall of the garrison. Colonel Rainborough's own guards accused each other of negligence. One of them who was alleged to have spent the night in a brothel when he was supposed to be standing guard, went south, intending to clear himself at headquarters. When he reached London, he was told he would be examined by the two Houses of Parliament, and detained pending this examination. He heard a rumour that he was to be shot and escaped without any difficulty, issuing a *Vindication* of his conduct and denial of the brothel story, printed in Amsterdam, the day before Rainborough's funeral.[103]

In stark contrast to the negligence with which Rainborough's murder was treated by the military and civilian establishment was the celebration of his funeral on 14th November by his family, friends and supporters. Fifty or sixty coaches and nearly three thousand men on horseback or on foot assembled at Tottenham High Cross and proceeded through Islington and Smithfield to Old Bailey and Ludgate, along Cheapside and Cornhill to St John's Chapel in Wapping where Thomas Rainborough was buried beside his father. The mourners, led by William Rainborough, wore sea-green ribbons in deference to the Colonel's sea-faring career and sea-green in place of blue became the Leveller colour in the future. The Royalist press sneered at the supposed social background of the mourners. According to one of the papers, all the professions were represented: Will the Weaver, Tom the Tapster, Kit the

70

Cobbler, Dick the Door Sweeper and many more Apron-youths of the City. Another Royalist writer remarked 'thousands of the Levelling faction went out to meet their dead champion ... while I stayed at home.' It is difficult to see how he felt so confident in producing an eye-witness account.[104]

The funeral sermon was preached by Thomas Brooks, a man forty years old in 1648, who had been chaplain to Colonel Rainborough's father, and, as he said, had served with Thomas himself at sea and on land. He knew the dead man well and was able to speak of him in genuine terms:

> When may a man be said to do gloriously? – when he does things others have no heart for, or are afraid to do, when he holds on, notwithstanding discouragement, 'blow high or blow low, rain or shine, let men smile or frown.'
>
> I need not tell you what discouragements the noble Champion met with from malignant pens, spirits and tongues, but through all ... he was able to do [God's] work and to serve his generation... It is nothing for a man to serve his generation when he hath wind and tide on his side.[105]

Radicals seldom have wind and tide on their side. It may be that this is something in which they are not interested. In view of Thomas Rainborough's death at the age of thirty-eight, at a crucial time in the history of his country, it is not possible to assess him as a leader. Opinions of him varied hugely among his contemporaries, as they have subsequently done among historians. The Levellers tried to see virtue in his end:

> What if Heaven purpos'd Rainborough's fall to be
> A prop for England's dying Libertie?
> And did Love thus suffer one to fall
> That Charles by Treaty might not ruin all?
> For who'l expect that Treaty should do good
> Whose longer date commenc'd with Rainborough's
> blood.

So noble Fairfax and bold Cromwell see
What honours are prepared for thee, and thee
Conclude a peace with Charles; you shall ride
Triumphant with your robes of Scarlet dyed.
Here lies as much true valour as could dye:
A sacrifice for England's true liberty.
Great and Good Rainborough (enough is said)
Through Cholmley's pride and Cowardice betrayed.[106]

(See Fig. 2)

The Commons ordered payment of arrears of pay to Thomas Rainborough's widow and provision in trust for his child or children. Fairfax personally wrote to the Speaker urging the needs of the family and the fact that attending to these was the least Parliament could do in view of the Colonel's gallant and faithful service to the kingdom but things moved very slowly. Twenty months after the murder, the Commons voted £200 p.a. to be paid to Margaret Rainborough until lands could be settled on her and her son, William. No evidence survives of such a grant being made. Fortunately the family was not destitute. In the 1650s, John Wildman, one of the two civilian radicals present at the Putney debates, now turned speculator, was able to invest £3,000 in property for Mrs Rainborough. After the Restoration, William emigrated to New England with his uncle of the same name, to join his uncle Edward who had been there since the 1630s.[107]

PART 2

Robert Lockyer c.1626–1649

I am ready and willing to dye for my Country and liberty and I blesse God I am not afraid to look death in the face in this particular cause God hath called me to. (Robert Lockyer, 1649)

Lockyer, an Agitator, spit in the King's face and cried Justice. (*Miranda*, listed in Sir William Dugdale's Diary 1649 – unpublished)

Robert Lockyer's story is short in comparison with the other stories in this book but then so was his life. At the age of twenty-three, without a blindfold and with 'a smiling conscience', he faced a firing squad.[1]

The first thing known about him is that he received adult baptism at the age of sixteen in 1642, together with his mother, Mary, at the hands of Richard Blunt of the Particular Baptists of Bishopsgate. It emerged at the time of his execution that he had sisters and cousins as well as many friends.* It sounds as if he had been brought up in a family group in Bishopsgate, a prosperous suburb which included 'many fair houses for merchants and artificers and many fair inns for travellers' but also 'many houses ... much pestered with people', typical of the jerry-building boom of the seventeenth century in London.

---

*The name Lockyer was a common one in the seventeenth century and there is no evidence that Robert was related either to Nicholas Lockyer, a leading agitator in 1647, or another Nicholas, a noted preacher and supporter of Cromwell's, or John, an active plotter against Charles II after the Restoration.

The inns for travellers included The Mouth, a tavern later described as one of the 'two new Houses of Parliament' of the Levellers who held meetings there.[2]

Radical religion led to radical politics but radicals, by their very nature, do not all arrive at the same conclusions.

> 'Men of sense are really but of one religion.'
> What religion is that?'
> Men of sense never tell.'[3]

This was a conclusion reached at the end of the seventeenth century, a time of defeat and disillusion for radicals. The Puritans of the 1640s and 1650s were gloriously deficient in this kind of sense. They were, of course, able to express themselves because censorship, rigidly enforced in the 1630s, had broken down. They were prepared to tell all about their beliefs. The numerous names – some of which are interchangeable – by which the various groups are known indicate the varieties of religion and religious practice possible during these decades. The spiritual journeys of men who claimed to have travelled from Anglican to Presbyterian to Independent to Antinomian to Seeker to Ranter to Quaker, or were accused of having travelled from Independent to Brownist to Anabaptist to Arminian to Mortalist to Seeker to Antiscripturist to Questionist to Sceptic to Atheist, illustrate the possibilities open to people who abandoned the Established Church. Saints – not a name of opprobrium but a name adopted by Puritans of themselves – were aggressive and confident. (Seventeenth-century use of the word 'Saint' bears no relation to its twentieth-century use.) Saints believed in the Millennium: a period of one thousand years during which Jesus Christ would rule in person on earth with the help of vice-regents – themselves. Their evidence came from the apocalyptic books of Daniel and Revelation and their hopes were increasingly pinned on the year 1656, or 1666, which matched the number of the Beast: six hundred and sixty-six. The believed that Christ's rule on earth would involve practical, legal and social changes, here and now. It was not easy to agree in practice what these should be although 'Saints on earth', the rule of Christ's regents, was a concrete and recognisable ideal for them.[4]

In the early seventeenth century, those Puritans who found themselves unable to remain loyal to their parish church, or unable to believe in the possibility of adapting it to suit themselves, separated into minute, individual churches of their own, small enough to meet secretly in private houses, taking responsibility for their own sick and widows, opposed to tithes and too poor to maintain full-time pastors. They supported the idea of the pastor's right or duty to maintain himself – 'to work with [his] hands as the Apostles did' – and the right of the congregation to choose and ordain a lay member of the church to act as pastor if need be. They did continue at first to feel the need to be a church, 'a congregation of Christians locally organised'. Such churches, with congregations which were identifiable and known to each other, as distinct from sects with an amorphous and constantly changing membership, had existed in London since the beginning of the seventeenth century and had survived withdrawals – to New England, for example, or splits as between General and Particular Baptists.* The collapse of censorship and challenge of a society in which all really was in pieces in the 1640s allowed for the subsequent development of sects, always a likelihood among religious radicals and rebels.

The first Separatists who formed churches of their own rejected infant baptism – 'the Scripture seems not to have clearly determined this particular' – but clung to the rite as the means whereby a committed adult could signify his membership of a particular praying community. On the eve of the First Civil War there were, perhaps, 1,000 Baptists in London out of a total population of more than 250,000, a number which was growing. When Robert Lockyer was re-baptised by means of total immersion, together with more than fifty others, his action symbolised rejection of previous membership of

---

* General Baptists believed in redemption for all; Particular Baptists remained attached to the doctrine of salvation for the Elect.

the Established Church and the death and resurrection of the individual soul of a committed adult believer. In political terms it symbolised rejection of the State Church and the support which it gave to the doctrine of obedience to the established order in Church and State.[5]

English Baptists, such as Robert Lockyer, were neither anarchists nor pacifists. They accepted the principles of war and military discipline and enlisted in 1642. Baptism spread rapidly through Parliament's armies and among civilians in areas in which men were quartered for any length of time. Robert Lockyer, sixteen years old at the time of his adult baptism, joined the army in the same year and found a large and growing number of Baptists among his fellow-soldiers, officers and men. In June 1647 a preacher recently returned from New England asserted furiously and nervously that the Army was mounted on 'Saddles of John a Leyden's make'. Contemporaries would have had no difficulty with this reference. John a Leyden was the leader of a group of radicals who seized power in Munster in 1534 and introduced communism and polygamy. Horror stories about this experiment abounded; Anabaptism, the pejorative term for Baptism, signified the breakdown of discipline and order and conservatives of all kinds reacted in alarm to the idea of Baptism spreading in the New Model Army. (The Leveller leaders, William Walwyn and Richard Overton, were unusual in expressing scepticism about the Munster stories, 'histories of the Anabaptists [written by] ... their enemies'.)[6] In the end, English Baptists themselves gave up their political radicalism for fear of a collapse of social and political control but a spirit of enterprise, directly attributable to religious fervour and questioning, was developing among Parliament's soldiers even before the New Model was formed. Sectaries, though assessed as only one man in twenty, represented 'the soul of the army' by 1645 in the opinion of one of their conservative, Presbyterian critics.[7]

Edward Whalley, Robert Lockyer's colonel and one of Cromwell's cousins, was 'called a Presbyterian tho' not of that judgement in several points'. His regiment, formed in 1645, incorporated the Ironsides, Cromwell's own troop in which

Lockyer first served. After Naseby in June 1645 Richard Baxter, the celebrated Puritan preacher and theologian, agreed to leave his peaceful scholarly existence in Coventry and become chaplain to Whalley's regiment in order to correct the soldiers and curtail the spread of error in religion. Baxter had been invited by Cromwell and his officers to become chaplain to the Ironsides at the beginning of the war. He blamed himself for refusing and thereby leaving the way open for the spread of radical views. He thought that he might be about to put things right in Whalley's regiment and remained with it, despite bouts of ill-health, until the winter of 1646. The soldiers whom he heard arguing 'sometimes for state-democracy and sometimes for church-democracy' were Robert Lockyer's fellow-troopers, and doubtless Robert Lockyer himself.*[8]

In May 1647 Colonel Whalley told Parliament's commissioners, appointed to sort out the problems attaching to the plan to disband the Army, that his regiment was swayed by 'Reason not Passion'. There was harmony between the officers and their men. Nevertheless Lieutenant Chillenden, one of the officer-agitators of this regiment, himself a Baptist, number 102 in the agitators' original cypher, played a leading part in the political manoeuvres of the summer of 1647. The regiment was more politically aware than its colonel was prepared to admit. It was one of the five cavalry regiments which appointed new agents in September 1647 at the instigation of John Lilburne and the civilian Levellers in London on the grounds that the original agitators, appointed in the spring of 1647, were now too much under the thumb of the Grandees. The original agitators were, in fact, still working hard for the Army's cause at this time but they were establishment figures to the extent that their expenses were paid, they attended the General Council of the Army as of right and they were listed by name in the papers of William Clarke, the Army's secretary. The new agents, though chosen by five cavalry regiments noted for their radicalism, were inspired and directed from London and not always obedient to orders from the regiments concerned. They had no official

---

* See p. 11.

standing in the General Council and were unknown to William Clarke when he began to record the Putney debates. In his notes the new agent from Whalley's regiment went under the name 'Bedfordshire Man'.[9]

At Putney Colonel Rainborough had pressed for a rendezvous of the whole Army. He hoped for general acceptance of the *Agreement of the People*. The Grandees had appointed three separate rendezvous instead: one to be held on 15th November 1647 at Corkbush Field near Ware north of headquarters, one to be held on 17th at Ruislip Heath near Watford to the north-west and the final one on 18th at Kingston, Surrey, to the south. The second and third of these rendezvous passed off without incident but the first was the occasion of an unsuccessful mutiny.* It seems that Robert Lockyer was present. His regiment correctly attended the Kingston rendezvous on the 18th. In November it was stationed at Hampton Court, engaged in guarding the King. In the confusion following the latter's escape on the night of the 11th, it is possible to imagine the temporary absence of one trooper going unnoticed. Ware would have been easily within the compass of a trooper's horse and a determined rider. After Lockyer's death in 1649 a supporter of his wrote that the 'Saint-like thirst [of his enemies] could be satisfied with nothing but his blood' because of his former support for the *Agreement of the People* when they murdered Mr Arnold at Ware. If Robert Lockyer *was* at the rendezvous and supporting the mutineers, he was fortunate not to have been caught and disciplined. Cavalrymen were tacitly allowed to roam at the end of a day's march in search of food and shelter but to be as much as a mile out of an established camp without licence was punishable by death.[10]

Whalley's regiment took part in the siege of Colchester during the Second Civil War in 1648. After the fighting was over, the Colonel actively supported the purge of the Long Parliament and the setting-up of a commission to try the King. He was a member of the Court and a signatory of the death-

---

* See p. 51.

warrant. By February 1649, once the execution of the King had taken place, the radicals in his regiment and elsewhere realised that they had been out-witted and cheated – as John Lilburne writing four months later said he had foreseen. The political solution of a republic had been adopted; it was obvious, as the weeks went by, that the new Commonwealth would make no concessions to the rest of the radical programme, outlined in 1647 and vigorously canvassed after the second defeat of the Royalists in 1648.

Fighting had taken precedence over politics. The soldier radicals' claim to a voice in the settlement of the kingdom had been necessarily put on one side while the Second Civil War was in progress. It was renewed in the autumn of 1648. Negotiations were proceeding in London while Thomas Rainborough was engaged in besieging Pontefract. The Army Grandees had, however, learned the danger of allowing the rank-and-file to be heard. These latter no longer had a place in the General Council of the Army (a temporary institution which existed for only ten months between March 1647 and January 1648) and political deliberations at headquarters in November 1648 were attended exclusively by officers.[11]

Civilian radicals, in the early autumn of 1648, were furiously active. A petition dated 11th September, addressed to the House of Commons by 'divers well-affected persons' in the City, Westminster, Southwark and Tower Hamlets, expressed distrust of the current negotiations between Parliament and the King and put forward positive suggestions for annual elections, religious toleration, freedom from pressing and forcing any sort of men to serve in wars, equality before the law, freedom of trade, abolition of tithes and abolition of imprisonment for debt. The petitioners defended themselves from the charge of communism – as they resisted the name 'Leveller'. They confirmed their belief in private property but urged 'some effectual course to keep people from begging and beggery in so fruitful a Nation as through God's blessing this is'. They asked for an examination of the duties of the King and the Lords, arrears of pay, an indemnity for the Army and recognition of its service to Parliament and the kingdom.

The petition was said to have 40,000 signatures* and was frequently referred to in later Leveller publications as an authoritative statement of policy. The combination in one petition of specifically military grievances relating to particular circumstances and the aftermath of civil war, with requests for individual rights and freedoms which are timeless, shows how far soldier and civilian radicals had travelled in eighteen months towards establishing a common cause.[12]

Two issues were to be decided in the autumn of 1648: the fate of the King and the settlement of the kingdom. The first was comparatively easy, given the unswerving and unshakeable conviction of Ireton that he must be brought to trial and execution, and Ireton's ability to sway the majority of the Council of Officers. There was some disagreement as to whether Parliament should be arbitrarily dissolved or simply purged of those members who would have opposed bringing the King to trial. In the event there was a purge: on 6th December one hundred and forty members were forcibly prevented by Colonel Pride and his regiment from taking their seats and so the way was cleared for setting up the commission to try the King. The second problem, the settlement of the kingdom, was much more difficult and resulted in defeat for soldier and civilian radicals.

While the Army officers were concentrating on the fate of the King, John Lilburne and his fellows were looking for a constitutional settlement. At first civilians tried to work with soldiers. Plans for a new *Agreement of the People*, a written constitution to supplant the one drafted by Wildman in the autumn of 1647,† were proposed and discussed first by a committee of Levellers, Independents, Members of Parliament and Army Grandees. This *Agreement* was then debated at Whitehall

---

* This figure, however much of an exaggeration, may be compared with the total strength of the New Model at this time, about 20,000, and the estimated population of London, 250,000.

† The first *Agreement* of 3rd November was the one debated at Putney and the paper proffered by Colonel Thomas Rainborough to Fairfax, Cromwell and the soldiers at Ware.

by the Council of Officers, sundry civilians and radical churchmen, with Fairfax in the chair. The apparent problem was religious toleration, or how much influence the civil magistrate should exercise in matters of religion; the real problem was the increasing distrust of radicals evinced by senior officers and the increasing preoccupation of those in any kind of authority with the question of the King. The document, finally submitted to the truncated Commons on 20th January 1649, was shelved by them without difficulty.[13]

The beheading of the King on 30th January 1649 shocked everybody – that is, everybody who had not actually steeled himself to attend the trial or sign the death-warrant or officiate at the execution itself. By the end of February the radicals had woken up to the fact that the King's death left the Grandees securely in control, with no intention of making concessions to anyone else. Lilburne published an address to the House of Commons, significantly entitled *England's New Chains Discovered*, and the four civilian radical leaders, 'commonly (though unjustly) stiled Levellers', namely Lilburne himself, Richard Overton, William Walwyn and Thomas Prince, were arrested by order of the Council of State. After Overton, Walwyn and Prince had been examined, Lilburne, with his ear to the door, heard Cromwell shouting and thumping the table: 'I tell you ... you have no other way to deal with these men but to break them or they will break you'.[14]

Cromwell was now taking the radicals seriously because of current activity in the Army as well as the spate of civilian publications. On 1st March eight troopers belonging to different regiments petitioned Fairfax, asking him to restore the agitators and the representative General Council of the Army as it had existed in 1647. Five were condemned by court-martial to the cruel punishment of riding the wooden horse.* The case of these five men was energetically taken up by the civilian Levellers. They were 'the five small Beagles', heroes of Overton's pamphlet, the *Hunting of the Foxes*, engaged in pursuing and harrying the Grandees from the time of the first

---

*For a fuller description of this incident see p. 148.

political organisation of the Army to the present when the senior officers had united behind the Council of State. This pamphlet, which is clear proof both of Leveller support for the soldiers and of the soldiers' political activity, was enough seriously to alarm the Grandees. Their reaction to so much as a hint of mutiny in Whalley's regiment, quartered in the City, a centre for Levellers, is understandable.[15]

The mutiny in which Robert Lockyer lost his life took place on 24th April, one month after the publication of Lilburne and Overton's attacks on the superior officers in the Army. Captain Savage's troop, in which Lockyer served, was ordered to leave its quarters in the City and attend a rendezvous of the regiment at Mile End at which it was to receive marching orders to proceed into Essex. Thirty men seized the colour from the Four Swans in Bishopsgate Street and bore it off to the Bull Inn nearby, a noted meeting place for radicals, where they barricaded themselves in. The captain called them to bring out the colour and mount but they refused. He himself attempted to carry off the flag but the men successfully hung on to it, Lockyer saying that they were not his colour carriers and that they had, as well as he, fought for the colour and all it symbolised, the other soldiers chorusing 'All, all'.[16]

Colonel Whalley and other senior officers in the regiment quickly arrived on the scene, ordered the men to proceed to the rendezvous and promised, in response to the claim that they were unable to pay for their quarters, a further sum of money. (In fact Savage's troop had received one month's pay on 23rd April and therefore should have had cash in hand to pay their debts on leaving the City.) As it was smugly expressed by a contemporary: 'Good husbands [that is good managers] need not have wanted money to pay their quarters'. Free quarter when the soldiers' pay was in arrear involved suffering for the civilian population, as was well known and appreciated by the soldiers themselves. Troopers had to pay for their horses as well as themselves and this came to just under half of their daily wage.

Whalley promised Lockyer and his fellows that they would receive enough to pay what they owed but the men tried to

82

get security for their arrears as well, which impossible demand caused the Colonel to bring discussion to an end. He ordered Lockyer to mount forthwith and, when he refused, with the support of his fellows, arrested him with fourteen others. The crowd of civilians who had gathered in support of the mutineers was scattered by Whalley's obedient troopers. Fairfax and Cromwell arrived in person on the scene and ordered all fifteen to be taken to Whitehall to be court-martialled. One of the fifteen was acquitted, three were left to the discretion of their Colonel, five were sentenced to ride the wooden horse with a carbine at each heel and six were condemned to death. The condemned men petitioned the General for mercy, admitting their fault and promising obedience in future.

Fairfax upheld the sentence on Lockyer but pardoned the other five. The General maintained that Lockyer's repentance did not agree with the defence he had put up for himself at the trial when, awkwardly for the Grandees, he had maintained that there was no justification for the operation of martial law in a time of peace, an argument which dated from the Petition of Right of 1628 and the early days of opposition to Charles I. Enraged by this, Colonel Okey accused Lockyer of inciting the soldiers to mutiny. The court-martial regarded him as the ringleader and treated him accordingly. He had popular support, too, among civilians and at this stage the authorities were more afraid of the possibility of united opposition from Londoners and discontented soldiers than of anything else. A group of women who had gone to Whitehall a few days earlier to petition for the release of the civilian Leveller leaders were hanging about outside the court. Presumably they had not taken kindly to being told to go home, mind their own business and concentrate on their housewifely duties. They greeted the soldiers as they came out from the court-martial, saying there would be more such men as the accused in other places in the near future – a prophetic utterance as it turned out since the Burford mutiny was less than a month away and not one to appeal to the Grandees. They said that Lockyer was a Godly man and the authorities were going to murder a Saint.[17]

On 27th April a strong guard of Colonel Hewson's regiment conducted Robert Lockyer to St Paul's Churchyard for execution. He said that he was ready and willing to die for his country and liberty and that he was not afraid to look death in the face in the particular cause to which he had been called. He was joyful that he could die to excuse his fellows. Death would stop his progress from sorrow to sorrow and he had a 'smiling conscience'. He was troubled by the fact that he had been condemned for so small a thing as a dispute over pay after seven or eight years of labouring for the freedom and liberties of the nation. He urged his sister to forgive his enemies and executioners, denied that he had been the chief mutineer in his regiment and prayed privately, having refused the ministrations of Mr Knight, the General's chaplain. To the end he believed in himself, refusing a blindfold and speaking directly to the six men who formed the firing-squad as 'fellow-soldiers ... brought here by your officers to murder me.' 'I did not think you had such heathenish and barbarous principles in you as to obey your officers in [this]', he went on. Major Carter, in charge of the firing party, was visibly shaken. Colonel Okey, who had already crossed swords with Robert Lockyer at the court-martial, lost his temper, seized the jacket, coat and belt of the condemned man and distributed these things among the executioners, who then pronounced themselves ready to shoot.[18]

The official line that this was a mutiny about pay, and, what is more, one for which there was no justification, is scarcely convincing. A dispute about pay would not have brought Fairfax and Cromwell from Whitehall to Bishopsgate with such speed on 24th April. The real problem, as Lockyer's friends recognised, was *what might happen*. The Grandees were terrified of a rising in the City in which civilian and soldier radicals would be united. Fairfax claimed that he had been very merciful in sparing the lives of the five men who had been condemned. Robert Lockyer, he said, *was likely to have made** a grave faction in the City and the Army. The

---

* Italics mine.

shooting of Robert Lockyer, so far as the Grandees were concerned, did have one desired effect: Colonel Whalley and the officers and soldiers of his regiment issued a declaration of loyalty on 14th May, confirmed by five hundred and seventy-two signatures. The regiment took no part in the mutiny at Burford at the end of the month and proclaimed its loyalty by wearing blue ribbons (Fairfax's colours) rather than sea-green and black.[19]

Lockyer's fellow-soldiers may have been terrorised into submission; his funeral was a tribute to the man himself and a political demonstration. A silent procession of more than three thousand people, civilians and soldiers, made its way from Smithfield through the heart of the City then back to the New Churchyard at Moorfields, where the burial was to take place. On the coffin, which was decorated with bloodstained rosemary, there was a naked sword. Six trumpets sounded a soldiers' knell and the trooper's horse, clothed in mourning, was led by a man on foot at the rear of the procession, an honour usually accorded only to a Commander-in-Chief. Sea-green and black ribbons were worn, as they had been at Thomas Rainborough's funeral five months earlier, Bystanders taunted the mourners with cries of 'Leveller' but no one took any notice. The silence and weight of support for the executed mutineer must have been very moving and an unmistakeable tribute to the man himself. The Leveller newspaper said with truth that this was a remarkable funeral for a person of 'no higher quality than a private trooper'. Quality, of course can be measured in a variety of ways; Charles I, it was said, did not have so many mourners as Robert Lockyer.[20]

A list of *Miranda*, portentous events which coincided with the King's death, was compiled by the dedicated Royalist, Sir William Dugdale, who was in London in April 1649 engaged in compounding for his sequestered estates. It included signs such as a bright star falling over Whitehall, ducks seen flying over the scaffold, the cure of one blind in the Isle of Wight, the cure of a case of 'King's Evil' in Dartford, together with complementary disasters affecting soldiers in Cromwell's home country of Huntingdonshire and a soldier who bragged that he had brought the King to the scaffold and then had his eyes picked out by crows. This list included the following sentence: 'Lockyer, an Agitator, spat in the King's face and cried "Justice"', clearly a satirical comment, the writer wishing to draw attention to the impossibility of justice attending the unjust execution of the King. Those who had opposed him might expect to perish in similar fashion. The fact that Dugdale chose Lockyer for his example, though, is indicative of the impact this particular trooper's court-martial and execution had on contemporaries of all political persuasions.[21]

After the execution, Lilburne and Overton wrote an open letter to Fairfax protesting against the exercise of martial law in time of peace. This letter was publicly printed: it contained a threat to the Grandees. 'It was not accounted foul play to knock Foxes and Wolves on the head because they be beasts of prey' – an argument which had been used to justify the judicial murder of Strafford in 1641. A *Petition* of women supporters, who may not have done their own drafting, was addressed to the Commons the very next day, 5th May. It concerned that 'valiant, religious man, Mr Robert Lockyer ... inhumanly shot in time of peace, contrary to the Word of God, the *Petition of Right* [of 1628] and Coke's *Institutes*.' Fairfax and Cromwell were undeterred by these comments. Less than a month after Lockyer's execution, three of the Burford mutineers were shot within twenty-four hours of being captured, after a drumhead court-martial. On the question of trial by civil magistrates as opposed to martial law, Colonel Hewson (whose regiment supplied the guard on the day Lockyer was shot) had observed: 'we can hang twenty before they will hang one.' He made this observation in February 1649 over the question of unwelcome petitioning. The Grandees were prepared to deal summarily with mutineers.[22]

The protest against courts-martial in time of peace became a standard Leveller tenet, consistent with the claim that soldiers were citizens in arms, but, of course, incompatible with the notion of a professional army. After 1688 the problem was solved by a series of Mutiny Acts which empowered the army to enforce its own discipline on volunteers and conscripts alike in time of peace and in time of war. It is not possible to be a soldier and a practising radical. Robert Lockyer, by all accounts a brave and attractive character, was shot at the age of twenty-three after seven years' faithful service to his country because of an insurrection which *might* have resulted from a dispute over some troopers' anxiety to pay their debts to their civilian hosts and also, it may be surmised, their preference for billets in the City of London itself during stirring times. Lockyer's death was a tragedy but the official verdict: 'As he lived so he died, A Mutineer' cannot be gainsaid.[23]

PART 3

William Rainborough c.1612–post 1673

The chief end of government is to preserve persons as well as estates ... my person ... is more dear [to me] than my estate. (William Rainborough at Putney, 1647)

William Rainborough, like many of his kin and Wapping neighbours, started life as a sea-adventurer, one of the 21,000 or so English men and women who emigrated to New England in the 1630s. His motives were typical. He had to make his way in the world and disliked the Laudian church and the political regime of the time. He had an adventurous and enterprising spirit and was following in the footsteps of family and friends. On arrival in Charlestown in 1639, he was immediately appointed a member of the artillery company, the local defence force. The following year he bought a house in Watertown. His younger sister, Martha, who had married a local Wapping man, Thomas Coytemore, had arrived in Charlestown with her husband three years before William in 1636. Coytemore was a very successful merchant, a 'right goodly man', so William started with the right connections. Another sister, Judith, came over and married Stephen Winthrop, son of the Governor. After Coytemore's death, Martha married the Governor himself, a man thirty years older than herself, as his fourth wife. William's brother, Edward, also emigrated and made his life in Massachusetts. There was, thus much to keep William in New England in the 1640s. He and his family were connected with the leaders in political and economic society yet he hurried home at the first sign of a change in the political scene there.[1]

A less distinguished soldier than his brother, Thomas, William Rainborough was even more of a political animal; his varied career illustrates some of the most vital and difficult aspects of the life of fighting radicals in the seventeenth century and some of the ways in which they reacted to defeat in 1649. Sadly, no picture of him survives, little writing and comparatively few of his quoted words. His character can only be assessed from his actions. His politics seem to have been very similar to his brother's – active, impulsive and frequently sympathetic to the underdog.

In spite of censorship the New England emigrants were in touch with the growing opposition to Charles I's Personal Rule in the 1630s. The Winthrop correspondence is full of veiled allusions to the state of affairs in England. Among other things, it includes a routine and rather boring letter from John Clotworthy to John Winthrop, Junior, the Governor's eldest son, written from Dublin, all about cattle and sheep for the colony, but, read with a 'casement for my secret mind', revealing dissatisfaction with current trends in the Church in England. The method used was to place a paper with irregular rectangular slits of varying lengths over the letter, thus transmitting a private message.

In 1636, a correspondent wrote to John Winthrop: 'There is a difficulty in writing freely. We, in England, are yet in the storm, you under the lee,' but correspondence was supplemented by direct news as there were so many sailings at this time between New England and Old. The fact that many had emigrated for political and religious reasons is borne out by the fact that such a considerable number were prepared to take the risk of the journey home as soon as they heard rumour of change and war. Parliament's cause was their cause. Return migration overtook migration: 'Since the year 1640 more persons were removed out of New England than have gone thither.' The ships of 1643 took 'many passengers, men of chief rank in the country.' By 1645 it was reported that 'some of our best military men [have] entered Parliament's service.'

The English Civil War was far from being a mere scrap between English counties or a split within the governing class in England. It was, or became, a genuine ideological debate and the attitude of those who left home in the 1630s and then returned – in some cases with their wives* – when war seemed possible is evidence of this.[2]

William Rainborough was in the van of those who returned to take part in the war. The journey home, west to east, 'downhill' as the sailors called it, was generally quicker than the outward voyage which, on average, lasted eight weeks. It was also more dangerous because of rocks and strong currents at the mouth of the Channel. William was safely back in time to take part in the Irish Adventure of 1642, sharing an investment with his brother, Thomas, in April of that year. (Both brothers had inherited property and money from their father, who had died in February 1642.) On his return, William married Margery Jenney, an Ipswich girl, like his brother's wife. The Rainborough family is thought to have originated in Suffolk, migrating from Ipswich to East Greenwich and thence to Wapping at the beginning of the seventeenth century. There was much communication between these two ports and the family probably maintained connections with Ipswich after their move to London.[3]

William Rainborough sailed with the Irish expedition on 1st July under Captain Benjamin Peter of the *Speedwell*, who was designated Admiral, and Thomas Rainborough of the *Zantman*, the Vice-Admiral. Benjamin Peter's half-brother Hugh went as chaplain. Like the Rainboroughs, Hugh Peter was one of the Winthrop circle, having emigrated to New England in 1635 and married a Winthrop connection. Sent on a mission by the colony, he had travelled home with John Winthrop,

---

* Judith Winthrop, née Rainborough, may well have shared the spirit and political attitude of her brothers. Born in Wapping in 1626, she emigrated and married in Boston at the age of seventeen or eighteen. Two years later, with her babies, she followed her husband, Stephen Winthrop, back to England. She joined the household of her other brother, Thomas, and was with him and his wife at Deal in May 1648 when they had the alarming experience of being evacuated and shipped to London by sailors in revolt against him.

Junior, in 1641 and remained to become a leading Parliamentarian chaplain and, eventually, one of the regicides. He and William Rainborough would have been known to one another.[4]

Among those who returned from New England to fight were four men who were later commissioned in Thomas Rainborough's regiment in the New Model Army, formed in 1645. Israel Stoughton had been a deputy in Massachusetts. As a young man he had been in trouble for querying the extent of the Governor's authority but was restored to office in the 1640s: he became lieutenant-colonel. Nehemiah Bourne whose family lived in Wapping and were connected by marriage with the Rainboroughs, himself a ship's carpenter who had crossed the Atlantic many times, became a major in the 7th Regiment of Foot (Thomas Rainborough's) and remained a loyal supporter of the Good Old Cause until after the death of Oliver Cromwell and the failure of his son. John Leverett, son of one of the elders of the church of Boston, was one of the captains, and William Hudson, an ensign. Israel Stoughton died in England, the rest of these men eventually returned to New England. Stephen Winthrop, who had been a member of the colonial legislature for several years and Recorder of Boston, went to England in 1646 and served in the same cavalry regiment as his brother-in-law, William Rainborough. He was followed by his wife and children and never went back, though he seems to have wished to do so and the poor of Boston were remembered in his will.[5]

The Irish expedition provided William Rainborough with his first and, it may be assumed, pretty uncongenial experience of warfare.* In September 1643, the Cessation, a truce between the Irish rebels and the King, was signed and English forces in Ireland were released for the King's service in England – or so the King hoped. William Rainborough returned to fight in Parliament's army.[6]

On returning to England, he headed for the West Country and became a captain first in Sir William Balfour's regiment of cavalry, subsequently in Colonel Sheffield's, serving under

---

* See p. 17.

Essex in the Cornish campaign which occupied the summer of 1644. In terms of establishing a military career he made a most unfortunate choice – in sharp contrast to his brother, who had the luck to serve in the best of the pre-New Model Roundhead armies and to catch the eye of the future Lord General, Thomas Fairfax, at an early stage. Essex was a noble character but a poor general and this was his least successful campaign. Even after the example of Marston Moor he was still attached to the idea of gaining territory rather than winning battles. He allowed himself to be outwitted and defeated by the Royalist army under the King, a surprisingly efficient general in the field, and escaped ignominiously by sea to London, leaving his army to surrender and negotiate terms. With mistaken generosity Charles I allowed Parliament's soldiers to march away, on the understanding that they would not resume operations against the King till they reached Southampton or Portsmouth. They had lost prestige, of course, as well as equipment and supplies; in fact the whole Roundhead organisation in the south of England had broken down. Those who were determined to win the war were inspired to devise a scheme for eliminating incompetent and half-hearted commanders. It was established that all Members of Parliament should resign from offices which had been conferred on them by Parliament. The Self-Denying Ordinance (as it was called) became law after anxious debate in April 1645 and ensured that Essex and Manchester, who could not, in those days, renounce their peerages and right to sit in the House of Lords, had to resign their commands.*

Essex wisely and generously suggested that regiments which had fought well in the past should be incorporated intact in the new army under their existing officers. His advice was followed by Fairfax, and the New Model Horse was thus formed from the cavalry of Manchester's Eastern Association, together with three regiments from Essex's. These three included Sheffield's, in which William Rainborough commanded a troop. The Lords objected to several of the officers

---

* See p. 22.

proposed for the new army, including both the Rainborough brothers, saying that 'it was inconvenient [for them] to publish reasons for [their] refusal of certain names.' The reason, almost certainly, was religious radicalism. William may have been tarnished by his brother's reputation; Wapping, where both men grew up, had a long-standing tradition of nonconformity and the younger Rainborough certainly emerged as a vigorous sectary in the future.[7]

The Lords' opposition was overcome and William Rainborough became a captain in the New Model Army. His regiment was stationed next door to his brother's in reserve on the right wing at the battle of Naseby, directly under Cromwell himself. The brothers remained in the same theatre of war throughout the summer of 1646. William Rainborough was involved in the siege of Bristol at which Thomas and his men won such glory. He then came into some prominence himself in the spring of 1647 when practical and, in some cases, political questions became important among the soldiers.[8]

In the spring of 1647 Parliament planned to break the New Model as an entity by disbanding some regiments and sending others to fight in Ireland under different officers. They ignored the practical anxieties of the soldiers, such as arrears of pay, indemnity for war crimes and provision for widows, orphans and the disabled. The Army perforce adopted a position of self-defence based on a united front of officers and men, horse and foot regiments and, in time, association with other armies under Parliament's command and with sympathetic civilians. They were responding to the wicked description of themselves as 'enemies of the State'.* Organisation took some months. The cavalry got going before the infantry. Above all, they had the advantage of mobility. Troops could communicate with one another even when their quarters were scattered over a considerable area, as they often were when there was a lull in the fighting. The cavalry were much better

* See p. 29.

paid than the foot-soldiers and came from a more articulate class. A cavalry troop, consisting of one hundred men, all of whom knew each other and knew their immediate officers, was a good size for establishing representatives, agitators, as they were called, to speak for the rest. When they were finally established, the agitators represented whole regiments (six hundred cavalrymen or twelve hundred infantrymen), four for each regiment in the New Model, two private soldiers and two junior officers, but representation at troop level had originally been contemplated.[9]

A series of meetings was held at headquarters in the spring of 1647 at which matters worrying the Army were to be discussed. Fairfax summoned a specially large Council of War, forty-three officers, most of them senior, to meet the Parliamentary commissioners. Unfortunately the initial commissioners were four of the Army's most dedicated enemies and they made matters worse by their arrogance and tactlessness. William Rainborough was present at headquarters from the second day of this meeting. His interest in Army grievances and matters which were soon to become political is thus evident from an early stage in the Army's political history, some weeks before he officially became officer-agitator to his regiment.[10]

He was present subsequently when the Commons had the sense to send officer MPs, Cromwell, Ireton, Skippon and Fleetwood, men whom their fellow-officers and men might trust. These four tried to be conciliatory but the situation had become serious. William Rainborough had clearly travelled regularly between his regiment and headquarters throughout April and May. He had obviously discussed matters with his own troop before the meeting which took place in Saffron Walden church on 15th May.

Senior officers had been told to discuss matters fully with the soldiers in their respective regiments and report the temper of the men to the meeting at headquarters. Thomas Sheffield, William's colonel, reported his men willing to obey Parliament's commands and to serve in Ireland 'with cheerfulness'. He was flatly contradicted by his senior captain.

William Rainborough explained that he had rendezvoused his troop by themselves and advised them to consider carefully their situation and the situation of their fellow-soldiers and not to be rash. He took time and trouble to explain matters and admitted 'many did not know what they did ... they cried out "Indemnity" and afterwards asked me what it was.' Not surprisingly, some of the soldiers were less sophisticated than others and needed to have their possibly dangerous position, so far as legal actions after disbandment were concerned, spelled out to them.

The Army's petition, described as *The Apologie of the Common Soldiers to the General*, published with an accompanying *Second Apologie of all the private Soldiers to their Officers* on 3rd May, had summed up six points: vindication of the honour of the Army (in view of the description of Parliament's soldiers as 'enemies of the state'), indemnity, provision for dependants and the disabled, arrears of pay, no impressment for service outside the kingdom and justice for the meanest citizen. These were reasonable demands but William Rainborough's colonel, Thomas Sheffield, was not unique in misrepresenting the temper of his men. Other senior officers did the same either by mistake or deliberately. This was the occasion on which Lockyer's colonel, Edward Whalley, claimed that his men were swayed by reason rather than passion.* Conflict broke out between the officers of Fairfax's regiment of foot concerning the attitude of that regiment. It was angrily reported that one, at least, of the cavalry regiments had not been adequately consulted at all. In the teeth of Sheffield's affirmation that his regiment was willing to serve in Ireland – particularly once they had heard that Skippon was to be in command – William Rainborough explained that *all* were determined on redress of grievances and an answer to the petition of 3rd May before they would consider future service. He added that the men had done nothing more than 'what became them as soldiers'. They could not be described as meddling in politics. Rainborough was sup-

* See p. 77.

ported by one of the lieutenants in his regiment, saying that many of the officers in the Army were as concerned for the good of the soldiers as for themselves – a palpable hit at the selfish Grandees. When the meeting in Saffron Walden church was over, the agitators of the eight regiments of horse, appointed on 28th April, issued a *Declaration* to the effect that some officers had wrongly reported dissent among their soldiers. There was, in fact, no dissent. All were united behind the published statement of their grievances.[11]

The agitators achieved much in the months following the Saffron Walden meetings: the securing of the siege train in Oxford, the seizure of the King and the setting-up of the General Council of the Army in the *Engagement* to which thirteen regiments subscribed on 5th June 1647 at the Newmarket rendezvous. For a time, officers and men, cavalry and infantry were united. Throughout the summer, William Rainborough was active as one of the two officer-agitators of his regiment with a seat on the General Council which he regularly attended. Unity was confirmed when one hundred and sixty-seven dissenting officers, including Colonel Sheffield, left the New Model in support of Parliament. One source describes them as being 'hooted off the field' at the Newmarket rendezvous on 5th June.* William acquired a more congenial colonel in the person of Thomas Harrison, a future regicide, who had taken the same line as he had done at Saffron Walden when he reported the feelings of the regiment in which he was then serving as captain. In the promotions which followed, William Rainborough achieved field rank as major and his brother-in-law, Stephen Winthrop, recently returned from New England, was given a troop in what was now Harrison's regiment.[12]

The Army had willy-nilly entered politics. It was driven to consider entering London, the political capital – crossing the Rubicon, in fact. The Generals, Cromwell and Ireton, wanted to delay this. They thought there was a possibility of getting

---

* See pp. 34 and 120.

Charles I's agreement to a constitutional settlement which was currently being prepared (later known as the *Heads of Proposals*). Cromwell believed in the existence of a party in the Commons sympathetic to the Army. He was vehemently and impressively opposed to 'getting things by force'. The agitators, on the other hand, pressed for a march on London. They had identified eleven implacable enemies to the Army among the Commons and noticed the dangerous concentration of 'reformadoes', unemployed ex-soldiers, together with the London Militia, a possible Presbyterian army in the capital. In the capacity of officer-agitator William Rainborough was present at the meetings at headquarters in Reading at which these matters were debated. His colonel, Harrison, was one of the signatories to the letter of 10th July, also signed by Thomas Rainborough, addressed to the City authorities, explaining the position and attitude of the soldiers and trying to assuage the fears of property owners.*

Within two weeks of the writing of this letter the march on London was precipitated by Presbyterian violence; the Palace of Westminster was besieged by a mob of reformadoes and apprentices and the two Speakers, accompanied by fifty-seven Independent MPs and eight peers, took refuge with the New Model. Fairfax was driven to take action; the City was occupied and the soldiers actually welcomed there on 4th August. William Rainborough was able to take up residence in his own house in Fulham and to act as host to his brother.

According to William Clarke's record, William Rainborough spoke twice in the great debates at Putney. It had been agreed at the end of the first day, 28th October, that a committee should examine in detail the principal matter of the debates, the *Agreement*, the radical constitution proposed by the agitators of nine cavalry regiments (including William Rainborough's) and seven infantry regiments (including Thomas Rainborough's). On the second day, after the prayer-meeting, Ireton made a long speech on 'this particular paper', which he said he was prepared to examine – on his own terms.

---

* See p. 35.

He regarded the *Engagement* of 5th June, drawn up by himself, as the definitive statement of the Army's position. The General Council of the Army, including representatives of officers and men, was concerned with negotiating disbandment, service in Ireland and such matters as arrears of pay, care of the wounded and disabled and an indemnity for war crimes. William Rainborough wished to widen the discussion, to consider 'the rights and freedoms of the people' and the extent to which these were guaranteed in the paper in front of the assembled company. The *Agreement* was read aloud and then the first article of the *Agreement* (concerning the unequal distribution of seats in Parliament in relation to the population) was read by itself. Ireton asked for a definition of the phrase 'the people of England' in terms of electors and was answered, in a way which horrified him, by Thomas Rainborough.*[13]

In the debate on the franchise which followed, battle was joined between those who believed in the intrinsic worth of the individual, as the Rainborough brothers did, and those who regarded property as sacred, conferring by itself alone a permanent interest in the kingdom and the right to choose representatives in the Commons. Cromwell denied the right to vote to men who owned nothing but their breath. Ireton said that a man without property, here today and gone tomorrow, could not possibly have a permanent interest in the kingdom. William Rainborough *was* a man of property but he claimed that his person was more dear to him than his estate. All native freeborn men should have an equal voice in electing representatives for their own preservation.[14]

William Rainborough was a member of the committee appointed to consider the *Agreement* and the franchise question and party to the compromise whereby the vote was to be given to all who were economically free, i.e. not servants or beggars, and specifically to all Parliament's soldiers. He was named to two further committees, the first consisting of eighteen names, to decide on what was to be offered to the soldiers, regiment by regiment, at the three forthcoming

* See p. 45.

rendezvous, and the second, a much larger body, appointed generally to consider the various papers of the Army and the *Agreement* to see how far they were consistent with one another. The second committee was immediately adjourned for a fortnight; the first worked fast to produce a practical answer to the soldiers' grievances with which Fairfax could assuage their fears and confirm their obedience. The *Desires of the Army*,* as they were entitled, consisted of a promise of immediate pay, six weeks if possible, if not, one month, these arrears to be paid out of confiscated Church lands (that trusty cornucopia) and Cavalier property, the end of free quarter and an increase of the monthly assessments by which the Army was sustained to a realistic figure which would cover support for the force to be sent to Ireland and the expense of disbanding the rest.[15]

The Rainborough brothers were 'young statesmen'. They were politically naïve in comparison with Cromwell and Ireton. Despite the fact that his regiment attended the rendezvous 'uninvited and without their officers', William Rainborough did not support his brother at Ware. From his own experience as a troop commander he would know how immediately the assertions, drawn up by the committee and read out by Fairfax, would match the most pressing fears of the soldiers. He knew how difficult political and legal concepts were for many of them. Ware had, of course, been inadequately planned in a very short space of time and its success jeopardised from the start by the King's escape and its probable consequences. William Rainborough may have thought it better to wait until the big committee had considered the *Agreement* together with the *Army Book of Declarations* (one hundred and sixty-three pages long) before presenting the former document to the assembled soldiers. In fact, an opportunity was lost for the radicals when the demonstration at Ware failed so lamentably.[16]

The disobedience of Harrison's regiment at Ware was punished by a reduction in its size. The threat of renewed civil

---

* Fairfax's *Remonstrance*, read aloud to the Army in 1647, was based on these.

war resulting from the King's negotiations with the Scots in the spring of 1648 was ignored by the civilian population which was not prepared to maintain an expensive and idle army in time of peace, and the senior officers used the opportunity involved in cutting down the numbers of soldiers on the payroll to rid themselves of political trouble-makers. Harrison's regiment was halved while other cavalry regiments in the New Model lost only about one hundred men each. Understandably, this provoked mutiny and three men, including one of the soldier-agitators, were condemned to death. In fact this sentence seems never to have been carried out. The reduced regiment served loyally under Cromwell in the Second Civil War, taking part in the battle of Preston. It was trusted with the job of escorting the King from Hurst Castle in Hampshire to London in December 1648 for his trial.[17]

In November 1648 William Rainborough marched in the van of his brother's funeral procession. In the funeral sermon he was mentioned along with the widow, other kinsmen and friends, urged to take comfort from the promise of a glorious resurrection of the Saints including Thomas. Four months later John Lilburne wrote grimly that William was receiving no help but rather discouragement in searching after and prosecuting his brother's murderers.[18]

It may be assumed that William Rainborough approved the proceedings leading up to the trial and execution of the King. His banner, ready for service in Ireland should his regiment be chosen, depicts the King's severed head and an arm holding an axe immediately below it. (See Fig. 4) He chose as his motto the classic justification for resistance to the powers that be: *Salus Populi Suprema Lex*. It is interesting that he selected a secular theme rather than a religious or moral one. Individual banners, most carefully designed and executed, proclaimed the identity of the officers who had chosen them, just as heraldic devices had done in the past. In the seventeenth century they were also a propaganda weapon, proclaiming what particular officers thought they were fighting for. The differences in design and motto reveal the characters of different men on the same side as well as differences between the two sides. William's standard reveals rather different priorities from Thomas's* and more positive commitment to the Leveller cause. Radical ideas which were scarcely current when Thomas Rainborough's colour was devised in 1643 had emerged in six years of struggle and become widespread – causing alarm and despondency to many but welcomed by a few. The idea of natural right, enshrined in the quotation from Horace chosen by William Rainborough for his standard, is an ancient one with which seventeenth-century men were familiar. Ireton at Putney had accused Thomas Rainborough of 'flying for refuge to an absolute natural right' and, in the process, denying all civil right. The first part of this accusation was true, although Thomas tended to base his arguments primarily on the Law of God; the second part involved the threat of anarchy, constantly directed at the radicals and their programme and recognised by Thomas Rainborough, who, by way of defence, reminded Ireton that property was recognised and hallowed in the Law of God by the Commandment: Thou shalt not steal. As things turned out William's standard did not go to Ireland. It survives as evidence of his point of view in 1649.[19]

A ballot was held to decide which regiments should serve in Ireland. Colonel Harrison's regiment was not among those chosen but two troops in it, Captain Winthrop's and Captain Pecke's without their officers, mutinied in support of Colonel Scrope's men who had been chosen by lot but refused to leave England, as they said, until the liberties of that country had been secured. They were joined by three half-troops from Ireton's regiment and supported by a private army directed by William Thompson, a protégé of John Lilburne's, cashiered from Whalley's regiment in the autumn of 1647. Men from a regiment raised by Thomas Rainborough's friend, Henry Marten, in February 1649 were also with them. There were

---

* See p. 14.

about nine hundred mutineers altogether and there seemed every chance that this number would grow. The situation, both actual and potential, was sufficiently grave for Fairfax and Cromwell to muster five regiments, a force of just under 4,000 strong, in Hyde Park on 9th May. They pulled sea-green ribbons from the men's hats and marched off in pursuit of the mutineers. Three hundred and forty men were trapped in Burford on the night of 14th–15th May, and locked in the parish church that night. A court-martial the next day condemned four ring-leaders: Cornets Denne and James Thompson, Corporal Perkins and Private Church. Denne was pardoned but the other three were shot in the presence of the rest of the mutineers and buried without ceremony in the churchyard. Colonel Eyres, cashiered after the Ware mutiny, was taken prisoner at Burford and sent to Oxford to await trial as a civilian. William Thompson, James's brother, was killed, fighting it out four days later near Wellingborough. These four, together with Arnold and Lockyer have been traditionally regarded as Leveller martyrs. The names of Privates Biggs and Piggen, executed in Oxford in September 1649, should be added to the roll. It is not a long one.

A recent historian has commented from his armchair: 'The Levellers were easily dealt with by the Army's whiff of grapeshot at Burford.' In fact the Grandees chose their victims with care. The executed had no social standing. 'Gentlemen Levellers' such as Captain Bray, Major White and Colonel Eyres, implicated in disobedience at different times, escaped with their lives. Radical officers whose men had been influenced by their ideas stopped short at throwing in their lot with mutinous troops. Of course this may partly be explained by a proper horror of mutiny among officers. There may also be an element of snobbery. Just as aristocratic republicans in the second half of the seventeenth century baulked at rebelling in company with lower-class Levellers,* so the gentlemen in the 1640s feared too close an association with the players. It is idle to speculate about William's true state of mind. The

---

*See pp. 138, 150.

evidence is insufficient. He seems to have taken no part in the mutiny but he did lose his job.[20]

Ten and a half years later, in December 1660, William Rainborough was examined in connection with a suspicious purchase of arms; he was then described as 'a major of horse but dismissed by Cromwell in 1649'. No reason for this dismissal is given, and the case was not taken up at the time by the radical press. The dismissal of a major by the Lieutenant-General may not have been regarded as newsworthy, but this was a major with an illustrious name and pamphleteers and reporters had been vociferous in the past about cashiered and punished men. It is true that the radical press had suffered a setback in 1649 when Gilbert Mabbott, a consistent supporter of the Levellers, resigned as censor on the grounds that current censorship was inefficient, censorship itself was wrong and licensing constituted a monopoly. Either William's politics or his religion must have been the reason for his dismissal, which must have taken place before August 1649 when Cromwell left for Ireland.

In the spring of 1650 William Rainborough's name was put forward by the 'Generals-at-Sea' for the naval summer guard. Although the Commonwealth was in control of England and Wales, Charles II had been proclaimed in Scotland and the Royalists held most of Ireland, the Scillies, the Channel Islands, Virginia and Barbados. The defensive role of the navy was crucial to the survival of the regime. It had to be greatly increased in size and re-modelled politically after the revolt of 1648. Continuing interchange between land and sea service was envisaged to ensure support of the Army, but William Rainborough was optimistic to think that he would be acceptable in Cromwell's navy. His Ranter reputation was against him, as well as his political background. The Council of State turned his name down for the summer guard. A purge of Ranters took place when the Blasphemy Act, directed against them, became law in August 1650. William Rainborough continued to believe in his own usefulness as a fighting man, and, it must be supposed, to support the Commonwealth for want of a better regime. In February 1653, when war with the Dutch was raging, he wrote to the authorities, begging for employment at sea and confirming his own 'zeal and affection' for his country's welfare. This request was turned down: the envelope marked 'Major Rainborough, spoken of as a very brave officer.'[21]

The Commonwealth established after the execution of the King was deeply unpopular in England. It depended for its existence on the Army, in which obedience had been secured by ultimate military discipline such as the best armies have always loathed in execution, and the navy, re-modelled and commanded by Army officers. Opponents included not only defeated Cavaliers and Presbyterians or the Roundhead right wing, but also the defeated and disillusioned radicals. Some took refuge in plotting against the government; this became more widespread as time went on, and included some strange alliances: others took refuge in wilder forms of radical religion.

By 1649 a split had emerged between political and religious radicals, Levellers and Baptists, a split which was seen by the former as a defection from the cause. As early as 1647 a group of preachers, including Thomas Brooks, who preached Thomas Rainborough's funeral sermon, issued a *Declaration* condemning equality and upholding the institution of private property. Christian equality, of course, involves equality in the sight of God rather than man, perfectly consistent with the institution of private property (which the Levellers also upheld) and a philosophy which accepted the principle of degree and everyone in his place in this world (which they did not). An open and bitter quarrel between the Levellers and the Saints developed slowly and painfully – as is always the case when former allies fall out. One of the Ware mutineers was escorted to his trial and imprisonment by an officer-agitator, number 102 in the original cypher, a leading Baptist who now supported the Grandees. A Baptist officer in the New Model, later executed as a regicide, arrested the Leveller leader, Richard Overton, in April 1649 and treated him with great discourtesy. John Lilburne angrily refuted the slander that he and his fellows sought 'to level all men's estates' but many were not convinced. (By contrast those followers of the Digger, Gerrard Winstanley, who established themselves first in communal settlements on St George's Hill near Kingston, proudly adopted the title 'True Levellers'. Their settlement was brutally destroyed by soldiers assisted by civilians.)[22]

In the seventeenth century few rather than most men could adopt a purely secular or material attitude to life. Thus some of the political radicals joined the new sects which proliferated in the 1650s. William Rainborough, a man of property, became a Ranter. Ranters were Antinomians, believing all to be in a state of grace. To the pure, all things are pure and there is therefore no need of a moral law for Christians. St Paul was confidently quoted in a general context which might have rather surprised him. 'There is nothing unclean of itself: but to him that esteemeth any thing to be unclean, to him it is unclean'. Heaven and Hell exist here and now in a man's own self. Whatever is done in light and love *is* light and lovely even if it has traditionally been called Swearing, Drunkenness, Adultery or Theft. (Clarkson did draw the line at Murder.) It is easy to see how dangerous this way of thinking could become in practice and the Ranters were ruthlessly persecuted between 1649 and 1651. They proved comparatively easy to eliminate because they felt no call to be martyrs; they were prepared to recant when faced with possible punishment. Some shocked themselves and turned to a life of extreme austerity while continuing to deny outward forms of belief and claim the operation of an Inward Light. Richard Baxter and John Bunyan both saw the Ranters as direct forebears of the Quakers. Ranters, visiting the Quaker George Fox in prison in 1655, called for sustenance and were sharply told by him that those who wanted to drink and smoke must do so in another room.[23]

Ranterism appealed to a disillusioned and subjected people who felt they needed a form of escape. Richard Baxter saw a connection between depression and the appeal of Ranter doctrines. Swearing provided an outlet for repressed emotions.

Alcohol and tobacco soothed the nerves and dulled the senses. Sex was also a possibility. A secret group, 'My One Flesh', with a characteristic greeting for one another: 'fellow creature', was formed in London and Rainborough was introduced to it by the charismatic Laurence Clarkson.[24]

Clarkson was a contemporary of William Rainborough's, originally an apprentice tailor, by 1649 an experienced itinerant preacher with several publications to his credit. These included a political pamphlet for which he had been paid £12 in 1647.* He had been born in Preston in Lancashire and brought up in the Anglican church. Rebelling against the church and the influence of his parents, he came to London to sample the varieties of worship available there. He moved from church-worshipping to the greater freedom of the sects and got into trouble with the authorities for 'dipping', or baptising by means of total immersion, as had been chosen by Robert Lockyer in 1642. Baptism in this fashion was increasingly frowned upon by the authorities as giving rise to sexual licence – particularly if it took place at night and men and women were baptised together. Clarkson reminded the committee engaged in examining him that 'nature has small desire to copulate in water'. His wife spoke practically in his defence, explaining that dipping in clothes would spoil them and involve the risk of colds. Shifts were provided, she said, for male and female candidates. Clarkson was released and spent some time as a chaplain, first in Colonel Fleetwood's regiment and later to a troop in Colonel Twistleton's. Quartered in Smithfield, he heard of the My One Flesh group and secured an introduction to them.[26]

As always, the government was anxious about what went on in London even if prepared to turn a blind eye to heretical and adulterous goings-on in the provinces. An Act was passed in May 1650 which made adultery a capital crime. This was not only a reaction to the threat of sexual licence among the

---

*£12 was a princely sum for a political pamphlet. A standard size, eight-page weekly newspaper sold for 1d and a Bible cost 2s8d. Clarkson had thought himself very well paid at Pulham Market when for a time he earned 20s a week as a preacher. As an artisan, a tailor, he might have earned 20s in a month.[25]

antinomian sects and an attempt to conciliate Presbyterians by demonstrating the concern of the Commonwealth government for moral reform but also the culmination of a century's legislative pressure consistent with a growing idealisation of married love and domestic life. It is repulsive to twentieth-century people who see sexual morality as a private matter. It is doubly repulsive in that it flagrantly upheld the double standard. Adultery was a crime when one of the partners was a married woman. Intercourse between a married man and a single woman was only fornication, involving the less serious penalty of three months' imprisonment. People cannot be made good by Act of Parliament and this Act was allowed to lapse in 1660. In any case it was drafted in such a way that convictions were practically impossible.[27]

Ranter writers recognised the Adultery Act as directed at their teachings. They quoted it, together with the Blasphemy Act of August 1650 under which they were regularly prosecuted. Blasphemy was defined as the affirmation that any human person was God and the affirmation that acts of gross immorality were indifferent or even positively religious. The punishment was six months' imprisonment for a first offence and banishment with prohibition of return on pain of death for a second – more humane than the Army punishment for heresy of a hole bored through the tongue, a punishment which was several times carried out. In practice the civil authorities were usually content to keep offenders in prison until they recanted, which was frequently soon – Ranters, as has been said, were not natural martyrs.[28]

William Rainborough was an atypical Ranter, a man of property and an office-holder in an impoverished group of individuals of a different social class from his own. (His father, though not his grandfather, had been styled Esq.) Evidence for his involvement with the Ranters comes from the autobiography of Clarkson, an impressively truthful account of a varied life, written when the author was in his forties and had changed his mind about many things. Clarkson and Rainborough spent some time at the house in Ilford which provided a centre for My One Flesh people and Rainborough

108

allegedly put up money for the publication of Clarkson's allegedly blasphemous pamphlet: *A Single Eye All Light, no Darkness*. Clarkson was examined by a committee of the House of Commons and an almanack (diary), picked up by the prosecution, provided information for the question: 'Did not Major Rainborough [sic] and the rest lye with other women?' As self-styled Captain of the Rant, Clarkson undoubtedly did, although sensibly and kindly reserving his money – or some of it – for his wife. Clarkson described Rainborough, among others, as a disciple. He cannot have been an average one. In any event, after examination by the Commons, he was dismissed as a JP in Middlesex – not surprisingly, since magistrates were responsible for enforcing the Blasphemy and Adultery Acts – and deprived of the possibility of holding this office in England for the rest of his life. Clarkson was imprisoned for one month and threatened with banishment, though this latter sentence was not carried out.[29]

His Ranter background and the hostility of Oliver Cromwell thus precluded any sort of a career for William Rainborough between 1650 and 1658. It is to be assumed that during these wilderness years he lived mostly in his own house in Fulham with his loyal wife. (General acceptance of the double standard meant that wives tended to overlook their husbands' infidelities. The generous behaviour of Margery Rainborough and Frances Clarkson was not uncommon.)[30] The death of Oliver Cromwell and the succession of his son, Richard, as Protector in September 1658 gave hope to radicals and Royalists alike. 'The generality of officers picked up their blood and spirits and came up to the superior officers to revive the Good Old Cause'.[31]

The Good Old Cause, a phrase conjured up by Henry Vane in 1656 when he was trying, in writing, to persuade Cromwell of the error of his ways, suffered from the old problem of division between the Grandees in the Army, the rest of the Army and those civilian radicals who had previously supported the soldiers. An expensive Army in peacetime was loathed by the civilian population and it was no longer easy for soldiers to claim that they were citizens in arms. The leading civilian radicals of ten years ago had mostly disappeared into private life, exile or imprisonment. A majority in the country, faced by possible military tyranny or anarchy, would undoubtedly opt for the return of the monarchy and the rule of law as preferable to either. The fear of some officers that Richard Cromwell was warming up the saddle for Charles II was, in fact, justified within a few months. Anarchy was the worst of all evils. Richard's supporters were prepared to support him personally only so long as he was able to keep order; once he had failed they began to work for the restoration of the Stuart monarchy. Richard himself had never really wanted to be Protector and not many people supported him personally, though some remained loyal to the name of Cromwell. The Protector's heir resigned thankfully in May 1659 after six months in office, spent a short period of exile in France and enjoyed the last thirty-two years of his life as a contented English country gentleman, successively under Charles II, James II, William and Mary, and Anne.[32]

After Richard Cromwell's resignation the search for a settlement of the country continued. A Commonwealth, or Republic, was once more proclaimed. The Rump, that is, those members of Parliament who had survived Pride's Purge in 1648, was recalled. Hindsight may suggest that the Restoration was an obvious consequence of the death of Oliver Cromwell and his inability to establish an acceptable dynasty. As has been said, some contemporaries realised this but, for the most part, Royalists were not optimistic in May 1659. Radicals are accustomed to a diet of hope. Agitators were active again, meeting at the Nag's Head tavern, inciting mutiny and discussing politics as in the Good Old Days. William Rainborough correctly saw a possibility of employment for himself.[33]

On 19th July, in response to his petition, the Commons appointed him militia commissioner for the County of Northampton. Three weeks later he was promoted to the position of Colonel of Horse for the combined militias of Kent, Rutland and Northampton. The militia, or county-trained bands, had grown in importance since the division of the country into eleven districts each under the control of a major-general in 1655, Cromwell's expedient to control the Royalists and other opponents of his Protectorate. Since the time of Elizabeth, the duty of every man to serve if his country was invaded, and the duty of men of property to provide armed horsemen in this eventuality, had been, in theory, regularised. This 'Home Guard' was expected to train and exercise but, with the honourable exception of London, the trained bands had proved useless in the Civil Wars. Experienced professional officers might be expected to improve their efficiency enormously. Competition for control of the militia developed between the various factions which were active in the summer of 1659, and William Rainborough might congratulate himself on having secured a significant job.[34]

That summer dragged uncomfortably on. A Royalist and Presbyterian rising in Cheshire was put down comparatively easily. The Grandees took control in the capital but the three leading Generals, Fleetwood, Desborough and Lambert, could not count on the obedience of their rank-and-file, whose pay was in arrear. There was no legal source of taxation and soldiers tended to take matters into their own hands when it came to collecting money for their own maintenance. Feeling against the military ran high among the men of property. It was said to be unsafe for officers to wear their swords in the City for fear of being recognised and insulted. The three Grandees were opposed by Establishment figures and radicals, civilians and soldiers alike. Over four hundred people signed a Remonstrance in November attacking the *coup* and calling for a second restoration of the Rump. Thomas Fairfax was the first to sign, closely followed by Colonel William Rainborough of Northamptonshire.[35]

In Scotland General Monck had his army paid up to date, re-modelled and under perfect control. He waited with his usual cunning to see how the wind was blowing, arriving in London with his soldiers in February 1660. He then summoned to Westminster all those members of the long Parliament who had been elected in 1642 and were still living. They were

111

summoned in order that they might dissolve themselves – a dramatic assertion of civil authority and reversal of the military *coups* of 1648 and 1653 – consistent with Monck's professed opinions in 1660 if not with his past actions. The Convention, elected in April, was overwhelmingly in favour of the return of Charles II. The King's welcome in May was such that he remarked that it must have been his own fault that he had stayed away so long: he saw nobody who did not protest that he had ever wished for the King's return. Monck was rewarded with the Garter, a dukedom and a pension. 'Some men will betray three kingdoms for filthy lucre's sake', as a contemporary observed to his face.[36]

The Restoration was a classic opportunity for jumping on to the bandwaggon. Many jumped – and were quickly disillusioned. The mood of the government became nervous and the populace less enthusiastic about the monarchy as rapidly as might, in the circumstances, have been expected. Informers abounded under Charles II as they had done under Cromwell. There were plots and rumours of plots.

In December 1660 William Rainborough was arrested and questioned about forty cases of pistols which he was alleged to have purchased. Twenty-five cases of pistols were seized at a house in Cripplegate and the householder, one William Waldegrave, said they were William Rainborough's property and had been sent to him to be sold. About forty men altogether, including Major-Generals Robert Overton and John Desborough, were questioned and imprisoned. This seems to have been a pre-emptive strike by a government jittery after only seven months in power. Ludlow, in exile, described the affair as 'a great plot ... pretended to be carrying on' and commented that the men secured were those who might have been useful in leading the soldiers and uniting the army if current dissatisfaction with the regime came to a head. The whole business had started with a disgruntled officer speaking out against Monck and the King in a tavern after the disbandment of his regiment and it is testimony to near-panic that such talk was considered worth repeating and worthy of action. The pistols may have represented no more than a punt, as Pepys heard Overton claim, but trade in weapons was, in itself, sinister, and searches carried on throughout the following year disclosed caches hidden underground.

While Rainborough and the others were in prison a disturbance did take place in London, the kind of trouble which might certainly have become serious with distinguished leadership and organisation. Thomas Venner, a wine-cooper who had emigrated to New England in the 1630s and returned in 1651, led an armed band through the City crying, 'King Jesus and the heads upon the gates'. About forty men altogether, rebels and loyal troops, were killed in the three days' fighting and thirteen, including Venner himself, were subsequently executed. There were fears that Fifth Monarchists* would rise in other parts of the Kingdom.

Pepys described the general alarm and his own terror but the King, himself, was sceptical of the danger and so was Clarendon. In February Margery Rainborough petitioned the Commons to examine her husband and allow him to prove his innocence, or to discharge him. The authorities seem to have decided that there was, in fact, nothing to investigate and William was released on payment of a bond of £500, put up by himself and a Dr Richard Barker as surety for his good behaviour. Overton and Desborough were less lucky, remaining in prison till 1671 and 1667 respectively.[37]

Rainborough left England for New England shortly after this. By 1673 he was living in Boston, where his brother Edward had settled before the civil wars and where his nephew, another William, Colonel Thomas's son, a former captain in the Protectorate army, also took refuge after the Restoration. In comparison with the other soldier radicals in this book, William Rainborough was lucky. He was the only one to die in his bed, and of natural causes, admittedly in exile, but in a place he had known in his youth and where several of his family had chosen to settle. His heart may be supposed

---

* See p. 138.

to have been in England, that is why he came home in 1642 and that is why he stayed there for so long without a career or prospects in the fifties. His Atlantic crossings were essentially influenced by politics: frustration with the regime of the 1630s; radical hope of overturning Charles I's government in 1642; admission of defeat after the Restoration.

William's character is full of contradictions. On the one hand there is the thoughtful officer, trying to explain complicated issues to the soldiers of his troop, spending many months in political debate at headquarters, the Justice of the Peace, an Establishment figure. On the other hand there is the reckless individual, abandoning his social position for a sect which appealed to him, throwing his bonnet over the windmill in no mean fashion. Perhaps the Ranter experiment was an aberration, a despairing reaction to the hopes and disappointments of the previous three years. It is to be hoped and supposed that he had learned to keep his mouth shut and to acquiesce in the prevailing illiberal climate of Massachusetts in the 1670s, even if he could not approve of it.

PART 4

Edward Sexby c.1616–1658

The wisest of men saw it to be a great evil, that Servants should ride on Horses ... The meanest of men, the lowest of the people have got the power into their own hands. (Memorial of Denzil Holles, 1641–48)

Against common Enemies, and those that are Traitors to the Common-wealth, every man is a soldier. (*Killing No Murder*, 1657, authorship claimed by Edward Sexby)

Edward Sexby, born in or about 1616, son of Marcus Sexby gent., apprenticed to Edward Price of the Grocers' Company in 1632, was described by Clarendon as 'an illiterate person [who] spake very well and properly, and used those words very well the true meaning and signification whereof he could not understand'.

Clarendon was speaking from a first-hand acquaintanceship with Sexby when the latter was in his early forties and negotiating with Charles II in exile during the Protectorate of Oliver Cromwell. He went on to describe Sexby's career with reasonable accuracy, saying that he had begun as a common soldier in Cromwell's troop and become one of those 'Agitators who were used to control Parliament'. Clarendon explained that a special relationship existed between Cromwell and Sexby. The two men, he said, were frequently bed-fellows, implying great trust on the General's part and a wish for private conversation from time to time in the night hours.[1]

Clarendon was both a snob and an intellectual snob; he was

115

seriously mistaken in thinking that Sexby was 'illiterate'. Sexby's writings and speeches show him to have had perfect command of the English language and a distinctive style. He knew Latin, probably having studied it at grammar school from the age of seven, and quoted freely from a variety of classical authors. If his schoolboy Latin had become rusty in later life he could rely on translations of classical texts; many were available in seventeenth-century England. Also available in translation was Machiavelli whom he regularly cited and once described as Cromwell's 'own Evangelist'. He was at home in both French and Spanish. Eight years after the Restoration of Charles II Thomas Hobbes thought that universities had acted 'as the wooden horse to the Trojans' in introducing dangerous ideas into the State; a cause of the civil wars had been 'the reading of books of policy and histories of the ancient Greeks and Romans'. Those who studied these works outside the universities possibly learned lessons which were even more subversive than those acquired by contemporary undergraduates.[2]*

That Edward Sexby chose to be apprenticed to one of the great livery companies at the age of sixteen rather than going to the university and the Inns of Court is symptomatic of a way of thinking which was not absolutely unusual in the seventeenth century. Primogeniture made paid employment essential for younger sons. The church under Archbishop Laud did not attract many, peace with Spain had curtailed privateering opportunities, there was never enough public office to go round and there was no regular army. There remained the law and trade. The Roman Law principle, which proscribed trade for gentlemen because of the corrupting power of money and because competition between gentlemen and plebeians might be unfair to the latter, never obtained in

---

*The number of published works which can be attributed to Edward Sexby is controversial. He published nothing under his own name but admitted authorship of *Killing No Murder*, using the name of a friend as an alias. It has been suggested that he wrote *England's Miserie and Remedie*, an important pamphlet, in 1645, and argued that he was the author of *The Case of the Armie* in 1647. Clarendon's slur caused historians initially to doubt his intellectual capacity but a revised judgement now obtains.

England and a significant proportion of apprentices in the City in the 1630s and 1640s were gentlemen's sons. Snobbery with regard to trade as an occupation only developed in the eighteenth century when the armed forces offered alternative employment. The Leveller leaders, John Lilburne and William Walwyn, apprenticed respectively to a clothier and a silkworker, came from backgrounds similar to Sexby's. Maximilian Petty, a spokesman at Putney, was his contemporary as an apprentice to the Grocers' Company. Samuel Barnardiston, son of one of the richest land-owners in Suffolk, led the apprentices who demonstrated in Whitehall in December 1641, incurring the admiration of Queen Henrietta Maria, who is said to have looked out of her window and exclaimed 'What a handsome young round-head'.*

All these young men suffered the same salutary culture shock – as it must have been. They were cut off from their social roots when they went to live in the City in the families of the merchants or craftsmen to whom they were apprenticed. They became men of business rather than men of leisure, wore the clothes appropriate to their new callings and adopted new hair-cuts – as caught the eye of the Queen. Their wits were sharpened and they acquired new values: 'No merchants are wrote Esq. but fools, coxcombs and cuckcolds', as one of them wrote. It is not surprising that so many were prepared to question the political establishment and choose their own heroes. The London mobs, deplored and feared by Clarendon, who demonstrated against Strafford in May 1641, stood up for the victims of Charles I's Personal Rule in the 1630s and consistently supported Lilburne, were largely made up of apprentices. Of course many were glad to down tools in favour of the sport of demonstrating but some acted from conviction. They came to London prepared for new influences and new ideas. They heard nonconformist preachers and read revolutionary pamphlets.[3]

Apprentices in London in 1641 claimed to number 30,000. In 1641 they proudly petitioned Parliament for the privileges

---

* The Queen has thus been credited by some as originator of the name 'Roundhead'.

of their order to be better respected. Actually a very small proportion of them could hope to make it to master-craftsmen. It was in the interest of the masters to keep a number of journeymen as wage-earners. An apprentice who had served his time and produced his 'proof-piece' or masterpiece had to find enough capital to start up on his own. Such money had to be borrowed and the risks were high. When the Levellers protested about the brutality and injustice of imprisonment for debt, the numbers in prison for this cause, the venality of jailors and the inadequacy of such treatment of debtors so far as their creditors were concerned, they were voicing the anxieties and concerns of the apprentices. In 1647 one of the requirements for Fairfax's soldiers, drawn up by a committee of officers and accredited agitators, read out at Ware and the other two rendezvous by the General, was cancellation of apprenticeship for soldiers. Once disbanded or 'demobbed', soldiers were deemed able to practise whatever craft or trade had been interrupted by war, and masters who hindered them were to be liable to fines. This was the plan of the radicals. Sexby's apprenticeship was over before he enlisted but this was not the case for all of the New Model soldiers. Cromwell as Protector showed real vision when he issued an ordinance to the effect that soldiers who had served in Parliament's armies for a period of not less than four years between 1642 and 1651 should be deemed fit to practise their original calling even if they had not fulfilled the terms of their original apprenticeship.[4]

Edward Sexby enlisted in Cromwell's troop in 1643 and subsequently fought throughout the First Civil War in Fairfax's own regiment of horse. It is strange that he remained a trooper throughout this period. Promotion in the New Model Army went, as the General once explained, by 'antiquity or merit', that is, long service or quality service, rather than patronage or privilege. Many men whose background was much humbler than Sexby's acquired commissioned rank. It is impossible to believe that such an intelligent and energetic figure as Sexby proves to have been did not distinguish himself in the ranks between 1643 and 1646. Perhaps his superior officers

Fig 1
Colonel Thomas Rainborough. After Gardner's drawing in the Sutherland Collection, illustrations for Clarendon's History of the Great Rebellion.

Ashmolean Library, Oxford.

Fig 2
Colonel Thomas Rainborough.
Contemporary woodcut illustrating
A New Elegie 1648.

Ashmolean Library, Oxford.

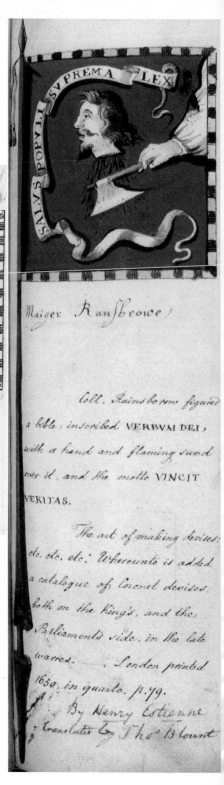

Fig 3
Colonel Thomas Rainborough's banner.

Fig 4
Major William Rainborough's banner.

Fig 5

Crossing Over. Dockside - detail from Wenceslaus Hollar, *Navium Variae Figurae et Formae* London 1647.

Fig 6

The General Council of the Army with Fairfax in the chair. The figure in the black skull-cap is probably William Clarke who recorded the Putney Debates. The bare-headed standing figures may be agitator representatives at the Council.

Rumbold the Malster and his man taken by five of the Earl of Arrons Milita,

Fig 7
Playing Cards celebrating the defeat of Argyll's Rebellion.

Capture of Richard Rumbold.

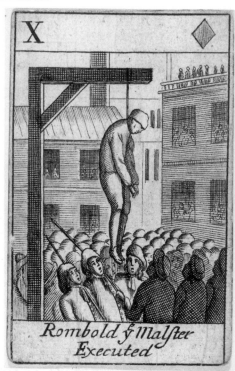

Rombold ỹ Malster Executed

Execution of Richard Rumbold.

feared his political views and his influence over his fellow-men. Early in 1647 he emerged as a leader and a radical plotter.[5]

In the seventeenth century prisoners were dependent on their families and supporters for food and drink and clean clothes. They thus enjoyed a window on the world. Out of the 'whale's belly' a voice could be heard – certainly John Lilburne's was. From the Tower, between March and July 1647, he published a series of pamphlets under the title *Jonah's Cry out of the Whale's Belly*, begging Cromwell to march into the City in peace, to deal with the King and to be wary of 'silken Independents', 'broken reeds of Egypt' in the Commons and in the Army. Above all he urged Cromwell to listen to the petitions of the *private** soldiers and the faithful agitators of the New Model.[6]

Lilburne explained that his information about Cromwell's current state of mind came from 'a knowing man out of the Army that came to me on purpose yesterday from the Army'. This has generally been believed to be Edward Sexby. Sexby's own special relationship with Cromwell has already been mentioned† John Lilburne, as he wrote in March 1647, was eternally grateful to Cromwell for the latter's support in 1640. As fellow-officers in the Eastern Association in the early years of the First Civil War, Lilburne and Cromwell had supported one another against their general, Manchester. In the anxious spring of 1647 Sexby and Lilburne may well have hoped that their old friend and leader would once more take the lead – so long as he led them in the right direction.[7]

Sexby was in the van of the movement by which representation of the rank-and-file of the New Model Army was, for a time, achieved. He may even have been its instigator. Agitators (agents) were first hinted at towards the end of March when

---

*Lilburne used this term, more polite than the seventeenth century's usual 'common soldiers', and one which remains current today.

† See p. 116.

the soldiers petitioned Fairfax and his officers about their arrears of pay. The soldiers asked for their grievances to be made known to Parliament and pointed out that there were few differences between the officers and themselves so far as these grievances were concerned. The plan was that this petition should be sent up to Parliament by two representatives from each troop in the New Model Army.

Troop level of representation which first seemed appropriate was then jettisoned in favour of representation by regiment.* Eight cavalry regiments, stationed within riding distance of headquarters, were the first to appoint 'commissioners' to 'agitate on behalf of their several regiments' and these sixteen men signed the document which Edward Sexby, William Allen and Thomas Shepherd took to Westminster on 29th April, the document published some days later as *The Apologie of the Common Soldiers of Sir Thomas Fairfax's Army*. Six grievances were listed: vindication of the honour of the Army (tarnished by being described as 'enemies of the state'); an act of indemnity; provision for widows, orphans and the disabled; arrears of pay; a guarantee against impressment for service outside the kingdom and justice for the meanest subject.[8]†

The Speaker had been reading another paper in the Commons presented by the officers in the New Model Army, or some of them, asking for the right to petition: 'as soldiers we have not lost the capacity of subjects'. The officers explained that they were trying to regulate the proceedings of the soldiers. They urged payment of arrears, a speedy end to the war and an easing of taxation of civilians. It is true that there was little difference between their situation and that of the men, as the latter had affirmed. The officers pointed out that they had left not only their estates but, many of them, their trades and callings, to fight Parliament's battle.[9]

Speaker Lenthal realised that the soldiers' paper was more alarming and of more pressing importance than that presented by the officers, ostensibly in its support. Fairfax had already

---

* See p. 95.

† See p. 96.

seen the soldiers' petition and Cromwell told the House that he had also been given a copy. It was decided that the three troopers who had brought it to Westminster should be immediately examined about its provenance.[10]

Sexby, Allen and Shepherd proved cool under examination. They were united in asserting that the document was the work of all. It could not be defended, as Sexby himself said, by any one particular man because it had been read and agreed, he thought, in each regiment and troop, meeting at various places. (Any hint of collusion between different regiments and troops, which would have been mutinous and treasonable, and which actually *must* have taken place before eight regiments could have agreed on the petition, was strenuously denied.) Denzil Holles (author of the Declaration of Dislike of 30th March)* and his supporters were outraged by the attitude and bearing of the three troopers. Writing after the Restoration, Holles opined that one of the three should have been hanged, there and then, by order of Parliament as a warning to the rest of the Army. Much future mischief could, he thought, have thereby been avoided. The Army's subsequent view of Holles in the summer of 1647 is hardly to be wondered at. He who had led the opposition to Charles I in the early years of the Long Parliament emerged as the arch-enemy of those who risked their lives and their livelihoods in defeating the King in the field.[11]

During the month of May Sexby was furiously busy organising representation and activity in the Army. He understood the importance of communications and the need for 'able pen men' to inform and 'undeceive' the people. John Harris, an actor who had set up a printing press in Oxford when the theatres were closed at the beginning of the civil war, began to print for the Army in the spring of 1647. Sexby had seen that the Army would be undone without its own press, and luckily there was one to hand, 'and workmen'. He urged an appeal to the officers for finance. In consequence Harris and his printing equipment travelled with the Army throughout

---

* See p. 29.

121

the summer of 1647 until September when, at the request of Fairfax, Gilbert Mabbott, an Army supporter, was appointed licenser by Parliament and the Army therefore no longer needed a press of its own.[12]

The political movement spread from the original eight cavalry regiments to the remaining two; to the New Model foot; to the army in the north commanded by General Poyntz; to forces stationed in Wales and to the seamen and Masters of Trinity House. Holles may have been right when he complained that servants were now riding on horses and the lowest of the people had thus got power into their own hands. The distances travelled and the energy of communication in a short space of time is impressive. So is the financial organisation involved. Foot-soldiers in the New Model were required to contribute 4d per head, half a day's wages, to a meeting at Bury St Edmunds in May. They wore red ribbons tied to their left arms as a symbol of solidarity till death. Poyntz was effectively removed from his command by his own men who proclaimed their loyalty to Fairfax. The seamen, as has been seen, were not impressed by the political thinking of the Army,* but the soldiers, officers and men, all over the country, were impressively united for a time. The success of the two *coups*, the seizure of the artillery train in Oxford and the person of the King at Holmby is scarcely to be wondered at in the face of such unity, zeal and determination.[13]

Edward Sexby recognised the need for funds for these enterprises. 'Tell the Officers they must disburse the money', he wrote in connection with securing the Army's press, and this, in fact, happened. Over £1,500 was paid out of the Army's contingency fund on warrants signed by Fairfax and audited by his Quarter-Master-General to cover the agitators' expenses in the summer and early autumn of 1647. Sexby himself was paid a total of £46 between June 1647 and February 1649 for carrying messages, several journeys, special service, contingencies and loss of horses. The horses supplied were clearly of high calibre, twice as expensive as those of the average

---

* See pp. 39–40.

trooper. That the agitators were officially reimbursed for the work they did in 1647 is proof that they were accepted by the military authorities, if not actively approved. Without funds they could not have been so successful.[14]

The senior officers accepted the agitators on the basis that this was the best way of controlling them.* (See Fig. 6) Timing and tactics were subjects of controversy in the summer of 1647. The Army had secured the person of the King – key to any settlement of the kingdom. The agitators remained deeply distrustful of Parliament and especially of Denzil Holles and the other leading Presbyterian members of the Commons. This distrust was mutual. Parliamentary commissioners who met five senior officers appointed by Fairfax at the Catherine Wheel in High Wickham in July 1647 refused to allow agitators or their representatives to attend the discussions – which achieved nothing. Later on in the same month agitators spoke vigorously at a debate at headquarters at Reading in favour of a march on London. They were not impressed by Cromwell's claim that they had supporters and friends in the Commons. Sexby said that Parliament accepted the New Model out of fear rather than love. He pointed out that those officers who had resigned their commissions rather than accept the *Engagement* of 5th June – the Army's contract not to disband or divide until its grievances be removed – were better treated and 'abundantly better paid' than those who had stayed. The fact that Parliament had sent commissioners to treat with the Army was itself suspicious 'for truly Parliaments or Armies never treat with friends … we cannot but look on ourselves as enemies'.[15]

The decision to march on London was taken out of the Army's hands by events in the capital and the failed attempt of the Presbyterians to seize power. Sexby, with the rest of the agitators, was quartered at Hammersmith in September 1647 when the Army established itself in the City.

---

* Colonel Rainborough was the only senior officer to express radical sentiments in 1647.

One of the agitators' demands in July, before the march on London, had been release of prisoners: 'Lieutenant-Colonel John Lilburne ... and all others ... in like manner wrongfully imprisoned'. In September Lilburne was becoming increasingly restless and increasingly distrustful even of his old friend and hero, Cromwell. The Lieutenant-General visited him in the Tower but he, Lilburne, had refused to promise that he would refrain from stirring up trouble, 'making new hurley-burleys', in the Army if he were released. His hopes were now pinned on the private soldiers in the Army and he strenuously urged the appointment of new agents because, he complained, the existing agitators had been corrupted by the Grandees and had become slothful and self-satisfied. (John Lilburne always translated personal grievances into public wrongs. He had quarrelled with William Allen, a leader of the original agitators, in the autumn of 1647.) It is true that the original agitators had become in some sense, establishment figures by this time – as is witnessed by the official payments they received. In September and October 1647 sixteen regiments altogether appointed new agents, sometimes called 'London Agents' because their job was specifically to work with the civilian Levellers in London.

Sexby was one of the new group, but retained his status as an original agitator with a right to attend meetings of the General Council. (The new group did not have the same status or recognition in the New Model as the original agitators. There was no question of their expenses being paid, for example, and they had no official right to be present at meetings of the General Council.) Sexby acted as a go-between, maintaining contact between John Lilburne in the Tower, the old agitators at Hammersmith and the new agents in London.[16]

Sir Lewis Dyve, writing regularly and optimistically to Charles I at this time, told the King that there were only six or seven men in the Army hostile to himself and enjoying influence over the soldiers. He said that these men might be won over. Three of them were named and Sexby was one of these three. Dyve's suggestion that Sexby might be soothed by the same arguments which had recently converted a leading Baptist minister to Royalism and that a prominent Baptist major and lay-preacher might be a suitable intermediary can be dismissed as fantasy, but his estimation of the influence of trooper Sexby in the New Model is surprising even when allowance is made for exaggeration. It came from knowledge of the man himself through conversation with Dyve's fellow-prisoner, John Lilburne.[17]

Soldier radicals and civilian radicals co-operated in October 1647. The debates at Putney which are justly so famous were not exclusively military debates, although a lieutenant-general (courtesy title) presided and the majority of the speakers were soldiers. Two civilians were present: John Wildman and Maximilian Petty. Thirteen years earlier Maximilian Petty had, as has been said, been a fellow-apprentice of Sexby's in the Grocers' Company. John Wildman, a young man of great ability (twenty-four years old at the time) but, as it subsequently turned out, few principles, was principal draftsman of the *Agreement of the People*, the proposed written constitution which formed the principal subject of the debates. Buff-Coat and Bedfordshireman,* representatives of the new organisation, the London agents, were soldiers but not known at the beginning of the discussions to William Clarke, assistant to John Rushworth, secretary to the General and the Council of War. They had not served in the Army long.[18]

Sexby was a vital link between the soldiers and the civilians. At the beginning of the debates he introduced the newcomers to Cromwell in the chair. 'Mr Allen, Mr Lockyer and myself are three' (all well-known to the Lieutenant-General) 'two soldiers, one of your own regiment and one of Colonel Whalley's' (clearly both unknown to Cromwell at this juncture) and 'Two Gentlemen'.[19]

Thirty-one different people spoke during the three days of

---

* Buff-Coat has been identified as Robert Everard, new agent of Cromwell's regiment of horse. Bedfordshire Man was one of the three new agents of Whalley's regiment of horse: Matthew Wealey, William Russell or Richard Seale.

debate – including the far-from-impartial if often pacific chairman, Cromwell himself. Proceedings were dominated by Cromwell, Ireton and Thomas Rainborough but there was an impressive degree of freedom of speech. Cromwell explained, at the start of the debate, that the meeting was for public business and that anyone who had anything to say concerning public business had liberty to speak. At the beginning of the debate on the second day, after the prayer-meeting, Buff-Coat, now known by name to William Clarke as Robert Everard, thanked the assembled company for giving him a hearing. Of those who spoke, twelve were senior officers, nine were officer-agitators, six were soldier-agitators, two were civilians and one was a chaplain. (Thomas Rainborough has not been included in this analysis because of his invidious position, appointed Vice-Admiral and deprived of command of his regiment in the New Model Army.)* Sexby is recorded as speaking five times and may have spoken more.[20]

He crossed swords immediately with Cromwell, whose reputation he described as 'much blasted' by the Lieutenant-General's recent negotiations with the King and with Parliament. Cromwell defended himself, and the debaters subsequently and commendably concentrated themselves on questions in the papers in front of them, eschewing personalities. Once the franchise question had arisen, Sexby followed Thomas Rainborough in supporting the right of those who had fought in the war to a share in the kingdom. Without that, as he said, 'we were but mercenary soldiers'. Cromwell complained that this speech of Sexby's savoured of will, that is 'self-will'. Of course Sexby may well have spoken truculently. In his next speech he apologised for 'zeal' but not for the point he had been making.

Do you not think it were a sad and miserable condition that we have fought all this time for nothing? All here both great and small do think we fought for something.

---

* See p. 43.

He was as decided as Thomas Rainborough on the issue of the propertied franchise. 'I think there are many that have not estates that in honesty have as much right in the freedom of their choice [of representatives in the Commons] as any that have great estates'. Thomas Rainborough, in his turn, stood up for Sexby: 'How should that be thought wilfulness in one man that is reason in another?'

By the third day of debating, Monday 1st November, the question of the King and the institution of monarchy had come to the fore. Cromwell continued to stress the danger of disobedience in the Army and the Royalists' belief that given enough rope the Army would hang itself. Sexby remained of the opinion that the Army had now a chance of securing the end for which it had been fighting. He was against setting up Charles I again: 'we have gone about to heal Babylon when she would not [be healed]. We have gone about to wash a blackamoor, to wash him white, which he will not'. ('Babylon' was a conveniently imprecise term for monarchy.) He aimed to put fire in the bellies of the senior officers, men in a 'wilderness condition', afflicted with blindness and confusion when they had a unique chance of achieving salvation – that is, a settlement of the kingdom on the basis of the *Agreement*, with a franchise wider than that which had existed pre-war, including those who had fought for victory, and capable of extension in the future.[21]

Sexby was one of the committee of eighteen, appointed on 30th October to discuss, among other things, the question of the franchise. This committee produced its report on 2nd November, upholding the sovereignty of the Commons, representatives of the people, in everything except religion, 'compulsion ... not to be entrusted to any human power'; the pressing of soldiers for any purpose other than the defence of the kingdom, and retrospective judgements relating to things which had happened in the late war. Some days later Sexby, Everard (Buff-Coat) and thirteen other agitators and agents sent an open letter to their various regiments confirming that the vote was to be given to 'all soldiers and others, if they be not servants or beggers ... although they have not 40/– in freehold land'.[22]

The radicals appeared to have won some important points but there were very few of them and they were up against very skilful adversaries. They were also lacking in luck. Neither Sexby nor William Rainborough supported Thomas and the others at Ware. Thomas Rainborough had been right when he feared that his party would be too weak at the rendezvous on 15th November. The Grandees were cool-headed and brave. On 8th November they judged the situation correctly when they sent the agitators back to their regiments to inform the soldiers of what had passed in the recent meetings of the Army Council and to soothe their fears. This soothing process was to be accompanied by six weeks' pay, or at least four weeks', and the assurance of regular wages in future. Fairfax, accompanied by Cromwell, reviewed the Army at three separate meetings, regiment by regiment, requiring the soldiers' absolute loyalty to the General and promising, in return, attention to their practical grievances. The Grandees were greatly assisted by the atmosphere of tension and nervousness which attended the news of the King's escape. Fighting-men recognised the likelihood of renewed war and the necessity of putting politics aside.*[23]

Edward Sexby, in his early thirties, now saw himself as a negotiator and politician rather than a fighting-man. Soldiering with his regiment had little appeal for him after the excitement of six months' plotting and planning. He therefore played no part in the Second Civil War but remained in London, in touch with civilian radicals there. John Lilburne, who had been out on bail, was re-arrested in January 1648 and sent back to the Tower. John Wildman was imprisoned in the Fleet. They had both spoken at a meeting in Wapping which was denounced to the Commons as a seditious assembly by a Presbyterian minister from Shoreditch. In fact they were supporting a petition in need of signatures before being presented to Parliament

---

*See pp. 50–52.

in which standard grievances of the radicals were listed, including the question of representation in Parliament, 'the Birth-right of all Englishmen' over the age of twenty-one who were not servants or beggars – the franchise which had been finally agreed on at Putney.[24]

Tension mounted between January and April 1648. Charles I was known to be scheming to escape from Carisbrooke to follow up his alliance with the Scots and to capitalise on the support which undoubtedly existed for him in Wales and Ireland and in many places in England. The London Levellers and their associates in the Home Counties and elsewhere were increasingly hostile not only to Parliament but also to the Grandees. Agitators in several horse regiments called for a revival of the General Council of the Army. The officers were afraid on the one hand of a Royalist revival and on the other of a breakdown of order. They sought an answer to their difficulties in a prayer-meeting, the traditional resource of the seventeenth century. Convinced of the justice of their cause, they then took up arms against Royalist, Presbyterian and Scottish enemies in Kent, Essex, Wales and the North.[25]

Victory was by no means assured for the New Model Army in the Second Civil War. In the final battle, Preston, it faced greatly superior numbers (combined, luckily, with greatly inferior generalship). The sieges of Colchester and Pontefract illustrate the determination and cunning of an enemy making a last stand. Army commanders faced treachery on their own side, accepted, if not actually encouraged, by their political masters in the Commons, as happened to Thomas Rainborough at Pontefract.

The Commons in the summer of 1648 were as afraid of victory as many of them had been in 1644 before the win-the-war party prevailed and the New Model was formed. A Leveller pamphlet, published in August before the news of the victory at Preston or the fall of Colchester could have been known in London, drew attention to the fact that the cause for which Parliament and the Army might be presumed to be fighting needed to be precisely defined. War is murder if the cause is not just. The author was clearly unhappy with a

Parliament of long standing which was unrepresentative of the people. He described the Army, by which he meant the senior officers, as aware of the need for a just cause and agreed reforms to follow victory in the field, but 'forgetful' of those who had spoken up for 'the Peoples' Freedoms ... [and been] proceeded against as Mutineers, or Incendiaries' – a clear reference to the Army's treatment of Arnold and the other mutineers at Ware.[26]

A disgruntled officer in Cromwell's regiment of horse published an attack on the Lieutenant-General, saying, among other things, that Cromwell himself reckoned that it was 'lawful to play the knave with a knave'. This is exactly what his own enemies proposed doing to Cromwell in the summer of 1648. John Lilburne was released by the Commons in the hope that he would be a thorn in the General's side. It was a hope which was to be disappointed. Employing Edward Sexby as his messenger, Lilburne wrote to Cromwell the very day after he had been let out of prison, confirming his support 'especially when you are low'. (Lilburne would have been aware of the Army's many enemies in the capital.) He went on, ominously, to warn Cromwell that this support depended on the General's adherence to 'the righteous ways of Truth and Justice'. If he were to decline from these at any time in the future he would find John Lilburne his foe, even 'when you are in your full glory'. Cromwell could not say he had not been warned'![27]

Lilburne and Sexby counted Cromwell a friend at this time, in spite of the fact that Lilburne had fired a warning shot across his bows in this letter of expressed support and Sexby had crossed swords with him at Putney. Actually it speaks volumes for the Lieutenant-General that lesser fry such as a lieutenant-colonel (retired) and a trooper should have regarded themselves in this light and felt able to write or speak to him in such frank terms. Equally impressive is the friendship which existed between Cromwell and Sexby from 1647 until 1654. This friendship is described by Clarendon,* based on information which he got from Sexby himself (who may well

---

* See p. 115.

130

have exaggerated) but also witnessed by the way in which the trooper was employed and the promotion which he was given. At Putney Sexby spoke as an opponent of Cromwell and the Grandees. He was reprimanded by Cromwell in the chair but the General must have noted him down as a man to watch, a better friend than enemy. He was employed by Cromwell to carry the news of the victory at Preston to Parliament. The Commons, as was traditional, rewarded the bearer of such good tidings with a payment of £100.[28]

Sexby was not a sufficiently astute politician to be aware, as Lilburne so quickly became, that the King's execution in January 1649, and the Commonwealth set up in place of the monarchy, had involved a betrayal of the radicals; that monarchy had been abolished with the tacit support of the Levellers but with no further concessions to the Leveller programme. In spite of the experience of the past two years he was still a young statesman. He may well have been seduced by the offer of responsible work and promotion. In February he was honoured with a commission from the new government to arrest the Scottish Commissioners who, outraged by the execution of the King, had left London and were making their way to the Hague to negotiate with the Prince of Wales. The accession of King Charles II had been proclaimed in Edinburgh on 5th February 1649, the very day after the news of Charles I's death had reached that city. The Scots (quite correctly) saw the execution of Charles I as the illegal act of an Independent minority, relying on the support of the Army. The Commissioners had charged the Rump with breach of the Solemn League and Covenant of 1643, suppression of the monarchy and House of Lords and countenancing 'ungodly toleration' in religion. In return, they were accused by the Commons of heading towards a new war. In fact, of course, civil war in the British Isles was not ended by the death of Charles I. Conflict between King and Parliament had widened into a conflict for the supremacy of England in these islands, and the opposition of Ireland and Scotland to the new regime was an urgent task facing the Commonwealth government in 1649 after the Army mutinies had been put down. England had to be garrisoned; given the chance, a majority of civilians at home would have declared for restored monarchy.

Edward Sexby was rewarded for his past service to Cromwell and to the State with a commission, the rank of captain, and the governorship of Portland in Dorset with instructions to monitor all foreign post. John Milton, Secretary for Foreign languages, had reported: 'One Sexby or Saxby offers how packets and letters may be opened and sealed again if he or his associates may be entrusted with letter-office'. The Commonwealth government were not prepared to go as far as this but Sexby was employed by Thomas Scot on sundry intelligence missions in Kent, Sussex and Hertfordshire. It may well have been thought prudent to keep him away from London or Army headquarters in the spring of 1649. A petition had been presented to the Grandees asking for the General Council of the Army, including representatives of the rank-and-file, to be reconstituted.* (It had not met since November 1647.) Lilburne wrote two highly critical pamphlets: the first and second parts of *England's New Chains Discovered*. It was advisable that Edward Sexby should be distracted, or bought off by military promotion.[29]

In 1650 he was given the rank of lieutenant-colonel and ordered to raise a regiment for service in Ireland. In the event, he was sent, with this regiment, to Scotland, and took part under General Monck in the twelve-day siege of Tantallon Castle in North Berwick in February 1651. In June of that same year Sexby was court-martialled in Edinburgh and cashiered. He was charged with executing a soldier at Morpeth in Northumberland without adequate reason and with mustering seven or eight absentee soldiers and pocketing their pay. On the first charge he was found 'not guilty'. Sir Arthur Haslerig spoke in his defence, explaining that the execution had taken place on his own order; if any one was guilty, he was, and the man had deserved to die as an example to others.

---

* See p. 148.

No proceedings were instigated against Sir Arthur and no more was heard of the executed soldier. Sexby defended himself on the second charge. He said he had acted in good faith and in the public interest, withholding pay from soldiers who were unwilling to go to Ireland. (Service in Ireland was notoriously unpopular and the Commonwealth government had already found to its cost how unsatisfactory it was to apply compulsion in this matter.) Misuse of the King's press was a common failing in the seventeenth century, either criminal and intended to benefit the officer in charge financially – as was the case with Falstaff – or negligent because the captain of each troop of one hundred men was also its paymaster with only one clerk to help him keep accounts. Sexby was charged as colonel, there is no mention of the captain in the absentees' troop. He may well have been framed. It was necessary to watch one's back in Monck's army, as a contemporary noticed. 'Almost every day, some officer or other is turned out or articled against upon some account or other ... Nothing is more frequent here than our officers exhibiting articles against one another: a man must have good footing that stands here.' Accused officers frequently resigned their commissions rather than stand trial. Sexby and another radical, Colonel Joyce (the cornet who had carried Charles I off from Holmby), accused of treason in 1653, both defended themselves unsuccessfully and lost their commands.[30]

Sexby was court-martialled in June 1651; four months later he was employed by the Council of State, sent to France with four gentlemen, promised £1,000 a year for himself and instructed to 'find out things, prevent danger and create an interest.' This was clearly an important mission of considerably more consequence than command of a regiment in Ireland. Cromwell had not lost trust in Sexby at this stage and was anxious to use his talents to the best advantage.[31]

In early January 1649, three weeks before the trial and execution of the King of England, the Queen Regent of France with her sons and her advisers had left Paris as a result of

133

rebellion there. Queen Anne subsequently described Charles I's execution as 'a blow to make all kings tremble'. 'The Parliament [sic] of France now taketh up Arms' wrote one of the Leveller leaders happily in March 1649 and a Royalist newspaper prophesied death for Louis XIV in the summer of 1650. Intense interest in political events on both sides of the Channel is not surprising nor, in fact, is it surprising that the English had very little understanding of what was going on in France. '*Frondeurs*', mud-slingers, the name given to the Paris rebels, suggested popular involvement and a possible radical character in the revolt, whereas the truth was quite different. Similarity between the names of the Parlement of Paris and Parliament at Westminster caused confusion – as is shown in the Leveller comment quoted above. The Paris Parlement was, in fact, a judicial body, a very different institution from the nationally representative body with legislative powers which sat at Westminster. Those *Frondeurs* for whom the question of arbitrary taxation, a constitutional principle, was at stake, needed to remain respectable and had no wish to associate with fanatics, levellers and destroyers of religion. In the second phase of the revolt, the Princes, Condé and his brother, Conti, and brother-in-law, the Duc de Longueville, pursued selfish ambitions of their own. Only in Bordeaux, a centre for Huguenots and an entrepôt for the wine trade, was there any republican and radical thinking – attributed by the Venetian ambassador in Paris to English influence.[32]

Mercurius Politicus, chief organ of propaganda for the Commonwealth and Protectorate, wrote hopefully of the 'English spirit' of Bordeaux and referred to 'French Roundheads'. What actually existed in the city was a brotherhood of artisan groups for mutual protection and assistance, 12,000 strong, aiming initially at control of local government. They were called *The Orme* because they met under an elm tree but it may be sadly relevant that the English saying 'you may wait for me till doomsday' is best rendered in French '*attendez-moi sous l'orme*'. *Ormistes* originally included Catholics and Huguenots who swore allegiance to the King of France but in time a Huguenot plot to declare Bordeaux a republic emerged.

The backing of English agents became important and the plotters were ready to play on English guilt for the betrayal of La Rochelle in 1628.[33]

The Council of State which employed Sexby on his mission to France may have suffered from appalling ignorance so far as Europe was concerned but was well-aware of the vital importance of 'intelligence'. A famous spy system was instituted under Sir Thomas Scot and John Thurloe successively. No cost or charge was spared to procure information for Cromwell, as Bishop Burnet wrote fifty years later. Sexby finally claimed £1411 13s 4d from the Protector after twenty-three months abroad. His mission had been quite dangerous. One of the original party of five was captured and tortured to death. An engineer, Joachim Hane, sent to France to spy on the fortifications of le Havre, La Rochelle and Bordeaux shortly after Sexby's return, escaped with his life after a series of hair-raising and graphically described adventures.[34]

Sexby's personal aims in Bordeaux extended far beyond the brief he had been given. He was well-aware of this himself and took to reporting progress, secretly, to Henry Marten as more sympathetic to the cause of a republic in this area than the Commonwealth government might be. He portrayed the *Ormée* as longing for aid. 'Oh England come and help your laws shall be ours.' He, in fact, presented the *Ormée* not with English laws as they were but as they might be: *L'Accord du Peuple*, a shortened version of the Leveller *Agreement* as it had been published under official licence in May 1649. This proposed constitution called for a republic governed by a parliament elected by adult males who were not beggars, reform of the law to reduce privilege, trial by jury and religious toleration, ideals which had not been achieved in England – as Sexby was well aware. Much of *L'Accord* was inappropriate to France and bore witness to hurried adaptation but a second section of the proposed document, the *Manifesto*, had been tailored to appeal to the Huguenot republicans, paying attention to trade and proposing equal treatment for all engaged in commerce. There was reference to 'our heroic princes' but, of course, these latter had no intention of supporting political or religious change, in Guienne. The final paragraph of the *Manifesto* bore witness to the Sexby who led the agitators in 1647 and spoke so eloquently at Putney.

No man is born a slave ... The peasant is as free as the prince, for he wore neither sabots on his feet nor a saddle on his back when he came into the world, nor does the king's son bear a crown on his head. We are all by birth equally free, and because we are so, have the power to choose the government by which we will be governed.[35]

The attempt to set up a republic in Bordeaux failed. There were not enough republicans: neither did a real leader emerge. Fighting in the city ended in August 1653 and Sexby returned home. Shortly after his return he addressed Cromwell as Lord Protector on the subject of foreign policy and the interest of England: 'Looking upon the interest of all the faithful in the nation, and myself with them, as being imbarked in that ship that God has made your Highness pilot of...' At this juncture Sexby appeared ready to accept the new constitution and Cromwell's new office.[36]

He stressed the advantage to England of possession of a town in France, La Rochelle, for example, as an 'offshore position' from which the French could be checked and trade prosecuted. An open attack on France would be very hazardous and expensive. Sexby favoured instead a top-secret expedition of English soldiers to be transported in ships recently taken from the Dutch, ignorant of its destination until safely afloat (reminiscent of the sealed orders opened at sea on the night of 5th June 1944), financed by Spain, whose ambassador had asked the Protector for an alliance against France, and commissioned either by Condé or the King of Spain so that there was no excuse for French retaliation in support of Charles Stuart.[37]

Sexby's project followed naturally from the missions of Hane and Sexby himself (ignoring the general lack of local support or sympathy revealed by both forays). It was seriously considered by the Protector but turned down in favour of an alliance with France, and the Western Design, a plan to seize an island in the Caribbean from Spain as a lucrative offshore base – Cromwell's most ambitious venture and greatest disaster, as it turned out.[38]

Sexby turned against his leader and former friend in the summer of 1654. In the words of the Lord Protector, he became 'a wretched creature, an apostate from religion and all honesty'. The same word 'apostate' was used by Sexby to describe Cromwell himself. From Sexby's point of view, Cromwell had betrayed the men he had led, surrounded himself with 'janissaries' and established a government as tyrannical as Charles I's had ever been. Many of his contemporaries saw Cromwell as a hypocrite, one who 'will lay his hand on his breast, elevate his eyes, and call God to record, he will weep, howl and repent, even while he doth smite you under the fifth rib.' Historians have exonerated him from the charge of hypocrisy and defended him as a pragmatist, prepared to accept other people's means for his own ends. There were, in fact, 'more warts on Cromwell's conscience than on his face'* but his own belief in God's providence saved him from doubt. He saw himself as leading God's newly-chosen people towards the Promised Land. Friends might be sacrificed on the way but that was irrelevant to Cromwell. Forms of government were but 'dross and dung'. He could not see them as other people's ideals. On the subject of the *Agreement of the People* at Putney he had asked: 'How do we know if whilst we are disputing these things another company of men shall not gather together and put out a paper as plausible perhaps as this?' It is not surprising that his former friends and supporters, unable to follow the workings of his mind, felt themselves betrayed.[39]

The Protectorate was generally hated in England from the moment of its inception. The Sealed Knot, a Royalist organisation, was in being from the end of 1653; its existence known

---

* The phrase is Professor Morrill's.

to the Protector's excellent spy-system. Fifth Monarchists – Millenarians – felt themselves betrayed by Cromwell, who was prepared to adopt their rhetoric but renege on the conclusions which might be drawn from its substance where tithes and the existing legal system were involved.* Republican enemies were divided between aristocratic and democratic republicans. The former opposed the assumption of power by a single person; the latter opposed not only the assumption of power by a single person but also the betrayal of those principles expressed in 1647 when, for a short time, the press was comparatively free and, as at Putney for instance, there were occasions when all could speak. There were times when aristocratic and democratic republicans could combine but they were few.

Fifth Monarchists and Baptists in the Army in Scotland were plotting against the Lord Protector in the autumn of 1654. In October three colonels in London signed a petition, probably drafted by John Wildman, calling for reforms in the new constitution. More than these three would have signed their names if the petition had not been prematurely discovered in the house of one of the signatories and taken away. Plotters had been meeting since September in the Blue Boar, the Dolphin, Mr Allen's house and Derby House. Involved with Wildman and the three colonels were Lieutenant Breman and William Prior, two of Sexby's companions among the sixteen original agitators of 1647, Captain Bishop, Alexander Pearson, Alexander Popham, Lord Grey of Goby, Henry Marten and, of course, Edward Sexby himself – a roll-call of

* Millenarians in the seventeenth century believed in the Everlasting Kingdom, foretold by the prophet Daniel, which would follow the four Monarchies of the Ancient World: Babylon, Persia, Macedon and Rome (currently represented by the Papacy). The year of the Beast, foretold in the Book of Revelation, was 666; hence, as 1656 approached, excitement mounted. When the Nominated Parliament met there were some who thought that the rule of Christ's Saints on earth, pending his own Second Coming in power and glory here and now, was imminent. When Cromwell realised the threat to social and political order implied by the practical ideals of the Millenarians, he commented: 'The issue was not answerable to the honesty and simplicity of the design' – and abandoned them, admittedly with more regret than he abandoned his former friends, the Army radicals, but with the same finality.[40]

138

the original radicals. The navy as well as the army was canvassed. Captain Lawson (later appointed Vice-Admiral), a very popular officer, was a friend of both Sexby and Wildman. These men were betrayed by one of their number – Francis Hacker – a future Major-General; many were arrested and imprisoned, including Wildman himself. Thurloe's reference to the '*vile* Levelling party', and Cromwell's speech to the first Protectorate Parliament in which he attacked the Levellers as self-seeking opponents of property and order, show that both men regarded their critics with fear and some respect. The radical cause was far from dead in 1655.[41]

When the February plot was discovered, Sexby fled to the west country. Doubtless he benefited from his own skilled horsemanship (witnessed, in the past, by his frequent employment carrying messages when speed was of the essence) and his judgement of horseflesh (witnessed by purchase of quality horses for transport of the agitators in 1647). In the west he had friends: a mistress, Mrs Ford,* in Weymouth and 'two high-flowne men in their principles, direct friends to Sexby and Joyce', Major Hardinge and Mr Waltham, also in Weymouth. Sexby had been Governor of Portland from 1649 till 1650, when he was succeeded by George Joyce, and Portland remained loyal to the radicals in 1655. The Mayor and Governor of the Castle arrested Captain Unton Croke and a party of soldiers sent to take Sexby, on the ground that they had not a written warrant for his arrest. Sexby thus escaped to the Continent. The atmosphere of suspicion and double-dealing was so great at the time that Thomas Harrison, currently in prison as a result of the plot, was reported as describing Sexby as 'a treacherous fellow' and a 'decoy for his Highness' (i.e. an agent for Cromwell), allowed, for this reason, to make his escape. Sexby never became a Protectorate spy, although John Wildman did, in exchange for his liberty after seventeen months in the Tower.[42]

---

* Mrs Ford may have been a common law wife. Sexby was joined in the Low Countries by a Mrs Elizabeth Sexby who bore him a son in late 1656. She returned to England to be with him after he had been taken prisoner and gave birth to another child. She was informed of Sexby's death on 15 January 1658 and consulted about the funeral for which she contributed 40s. This took place decently in the grounds of the Tower.

Sexby fled from Portland to the Netherlands, where he became acquainted with exiled Royalists – in despair because of the failure of the Royalist rising against the Protectorate in Wiltshire in March 1655. The leader of this rising, John Penruddock, was executed in May at Exeter. An enemy of my enemy is my friend, and the Royalist, Colonel Robert Phelipps, reported from Antwerp in May 1655 that he had 'fallen into an acquaintance with a most eminent Leveller' ... 'the principal man of that faction now out of Cromwell's power'. Phelipps explained in a second letter that he was giving 'my Leveller' full liberty to discuss English affairs since contradiction 'might have made him 'shy and reserved'. According to Phelipps, at this time Sexby was prepared to accept the King provided that the people were assured of their liberties and property (he admitted the difficulty which would emerge over ownership of royal and episcopal lands). He was not prepared to hold out false hopes to the King and described Oliver Cromwell as a 'false, perjured rogue'. Phelipps was understandably anxious to have instructions as to the best treatment of Sexby. A fellow Royalist confirmed: 'Sexby may well be a knave for ought I know ... but he is no fool.'[43]

Sexby was in communication with the Spanish commander-in-chief in the Netherlands, Count Fuensaldagna, as well as the English Royalists. He betrayed the Western Design to the Spaniards (the fleet had sailed in December 1654) and offered to organise a mutiny in the navy in return for £150,000. He bluffed his way to Madrid to persuade the Spanish government to supply money and a Spanish force to overturn the Protectorate, promising help from the English fleet under Lawson, twenty thousand English soldiers and the garrison at Portsmouth. These were desperate measures: they illustrate the depth of Sexby's despair with Cromwell and the Protectorate. The exiled Royalists knew of Sexby's journeys (he was known to have visited Madrid, San Sebastian and Rome in the summer of 1655) and of his negotiations with the Spaniards but felt no confidence in his motives. They feared (rightly) that Sexby was more concerned with eliminating Cromwell than with restoring Charles II.[44]

He was back in the Netherlands in November 1655, obsessed by the need to bring down the Protectorate. This obsession and the need to live in hiding, perpetually in disguise and under assumed names, told on Sexby's spirits. He was secretive about his Spanish mission. The old Leveller Richard Overton described him as 'very peevish'. Silas Titus, an officer in the Roundhead army now turned Royalist and living in Antwerp, said that he was 'morose and untractable'. The atmosphere of suspicion and mistrust among Leveller and Royalist exiles was enough to try anyone's nerves and clearly Sexby was never happy over negotiating with the Royalists. When there was talk of a meeting between himself and Charles II he asked to be dispensed from kneeling in the King's presence 'because that is Idolatry'. A soothing message came back to the effect that he need neither kneel nor kiss the King's hand if he did not want to do so. The meeting actually never took place.[45]

The one man Sexby wholeheartedly trusted was John Wildman. In May 1656, by the hand of a servant of Wildman's who had escaped from England the previous year, Sexby got a letter through to the prisoner in the Tower, cheering him up and asking for a cypher, assuring him that plans were afoot to bring about the fall of the 'apostate' (Cromwell). This letter, and a second, written ten days later, were both in Thurloe's hands by the beginning of July. It is hardly a coincidence that John Wildman obtained three months' liberty on bail of £1,000 on the first of that month. He was prepared to act as a double agent, spying for Thurloe on the one hand and plotting with Sexby for Cromwell's downfall on the other. It is claimed that Wildman never passed anything of value on to Cromwell's ministers and there is no hard evidence that it was he who betrayed Sexby in July 1657. Someone did, however, and suspicion remains.[46]

The Protectorate, as was recognised by its opponents in 1656 and proved in 1658, depended on the life of Oliver Cromwell. In June 1656 Edward Sexby paid a secret visit to England to plan the murder of the Protector. He recognised the need not only for propaganda but also for funds. Wildman was advised to distribute the Spanish money in his and Sexby's possession among the discontented soldiers: 'Money will not only gain the bodies but the souls of men'. Sexby had shown the same practical streak in connection with establishing the Army's press in early 1647.[47]

In September 1656 Miles Sindercombe was appointed first murderer. He was an old campaigner, one of the ringleaders in the mutiny of May 1649 who had successfully escaped punishment and enlisted in a new regiment. In 1654 he acted as an Agent to several regiments in Scotland plotting against the Protector. In London he was associated with another old soldier named John Cecil and a shadowy figure who went by the name of 'Boyes' and *may* have been Richard Overton, the Leveller, a former actor and adept at disguises, all part of Sexby's organisation. John Toop, a member of Cromwell's Lifeguard, provided information about the Protector's movements. The first plan was to shoot Cromwell as he went to open the second Parliament of the Protectorate on 17th September 1656. A room was hired in King Street through the windows of which it would have been possible to fire as Cromwell passed in his coach. The weapons had actually been taken into the house in a viol case but lack of an escape route discouraged the plotters from carrying out their plan at the last moment. A 'Major Wood' who may have been 'Boyes' himself, reported to the Royalists in Amsterdam that if Sexby had been there in person he might have pulled it off.[48]

The assassins' next idea was to shoot Cromwell as he rode from London to Hampton Court, his usual weekend retreat. This was a carefully arranged plan, involving sophisticated weapons and the acquisition of a convenient house from which they could be fired. Toop was to inform the murderers of Cromwell's place in the coach in order that they should be certain of hitting him. But the Protector gave up his normal visits to Hampton Court during the autumn because the sitting of Parliament kept him so busy in London. His practice, instead, was to take the air from time to time in Kensington or Hyde Park and

Sindercombe accordingly decided to shoot him there. Toop was still available to provide information about the Protector's movements and Cecil to act as Sindercombe's accomplice. Getaway horses were organised with a certain amount of wheeling and dealing, buying and selling in order to be sure of the best. These emerged as a bay from Lord Salisbury's stable, costing £80, and a black Morgan from Carshalton, bought for £75. (These were *enormous* sums. Special horses for the agitators, Sexby and Allen, had been purchased for £10 apiece when an average trooper's horse cost £5). Money for horse-dealing was supplied to Sindercombe by Sexby who confessed to having paid £500 towards the expenses of the plot.

There was a moment when it nearly came off. Cromwell, the cavalryman in him dying hard, got out of his coach in Hyde Park to admire John Cecil's horse, the black, and ask who owned him. Sindercombe was waiting just outside the park, the hinges of one of the gates had been filed nearly through and the palings cut to make escape easy. In spite of the season Cecil was wearing thin clothes in order to make himself lighter. The bay and the black could out-gallop and out-stay any horse in the kingdom. Cecil could have shot the Protector at point-blank range but his nerve failed him: 'the black horse had a cold that day' and the operation was postponed.[49]

The next plan was to blow up Whitehall – not exactly original – but in this case the incendiarists chose the chapel for their attack. Toop turned King's Evidence, Cecil confessed and Sindercombe was tried and condemned. He had, at one time, been apprenticed to a surgeon near St Catherine's at the Tower and thus knew about medicines and poisons which knowledge enabled him successfully to take his own life.* His suicide note asserted: 'I do not fear for my life, but do trust God with my soul' a bold claim in view of contemporary attitudes to the crimes of attempted murder and killing oneself.[50]

---

* Sindercombe's suicide was queried by contemporaries, Sexby among them, and has been questioned by historians. There are discrepancies in the story but the coroner's verdict does seem the most likely. Sexby subsequently withdrew his allegation that Sindercombe had been smothered by his gaolers.

Three hundred copies of a pamphlet entitled *Killing No Murder* were seized in London on 15th May 1657, and fourteen hundred more two days later. Two men were arrested and imprisoned for handling this cargo. Authorship of the pamphlet was claimed by Edward Sexby when he was in the Tower in October 1657. After the Restoration, when it was safe and popular to appear as an enemy of Cromwell's, authorship was claimed by Colonel Silas Titus, a former Parliamentarian soldier who had transferred to Charles I's service, been with him in Carisbrooke and subsequently acted as a go-between for the Royalists in France and the London Presbyterians. His pseudonym was 'John Jennings' and Sexby was suspicious of him for 'sticking so close to the King'. When printed in 1748, the pamphlet was described as 'by Colonel Titus alias William Allen'.* A nineteenth-century commentator dismissed Sexby's claim on the ground that an 'illiterate', as Clarendon had described him, could scarcely have composed 'that most able, logical, artificially constructed and occasionally eloquent treatise'.

There is, in fact, no reason to suppose that Sexby was not the principal author. The writer, addressing Cromwell, explained that he 'was one that was once ... amongst you and will be so again, when you dare be as you were'. This description fits Sexby much better than Titus. The Scriptural authorities, classical texts and quotations from Machiavelli would all have been known to him.† Hatred of Cromwell, a lost leader, leaps off the page and no one felt this hatred more keenly than Sexby, a former friend. William Allen, original agitator and close associate of Sexby, whose name was appended to *Killing No Murder*, was examined in connection with the pamphlet and told Cromwell that he could not have written it himself but boldly added that he would have done so if he could.

Killing No Murder justified the attack on Cromwell's life

---

* Colonel Titus certainly supplied the additions to be found in the second edition of *Killing No Murder*, acquired by Thomason in June 1659, by which time both Cromwell and Sexby were dead.

† See p. 116.

because the Protector had become two kinds of tyrant: he had no right to govern and his government was tyrannical. Assemblies were not tolerated, not so much as horseracing, wars were engaged in to divert and busy the people, a pretended love of God and religion had proved more expensive than tithes 'which now cost us all'. The need for a better society involves the need for laws but a tyrant puts himself above laws. 'Against common Enemies, and those that are Traitors to the Commonwealth, every Man is a soldier'. Furious wit is evident in the dedication – to Oliver Cromwell himself, whose death might undo the evils of his life and justly entitle him to be known as 'the Deliverer of his country'.[51]

Sexby continued with plots to eliminate the Protector. 'I have more irons in the fire for Cromwell than one ... either I or Cromwell must perish'. Colonel Titus described him at this time as much altered, moody but 'still sanguine', which Titus thought was either put on or mad. Cromwell's position actually strengthened in the spring of 1657. He refused the title of King, offered to him by Parliament in April, but agreed, in the following month, to nominate his successor and an 'Other House' of forty members. Republicans could still regard him as an apostate but it was more difficult to castigate him as an usurper. As Thurloe put it, 'the case was altered, Parliament having settled the government upon him'. (This was, of course, a purged and unrepresentative Parliament.) Titus was not convinced that Sexby could divide the Army against Cromwell. Sexby himself expressed confidence in the fleet under Vice-Admiral Lawson, a very popular officer and 'totally governed by [himself] and Wildman.' In the summer of 1657 Sexby came to England, in disguise as usual, but his movements were known to Thurloe. He had been betrayed both in Holland and England and was taken prisoner on 24th July just as he was embarking for the Low Countries, 'in a very mean habit, and with an overgrown beard'. After a short examination by Cromwell, he was sent to the Tower.[52]

John Barkstead, Governor of the Tower, a regicide and former Major-General, was ordered to keep him 'close prisoner'. Sexby's 'confession' was published in October. He admitted supplying Sindercombe with money and arms, negotiating with 'Charles Stuart' and receiving money from Spain. 'He was unwilling to discover anything further' – in other words determined not to betray any of his associates in England or in exile. He died in early January, aged forty-two or there-abouts 'stark mad' according to *Mercurius Politicus*, the official organ of the Protectorate government. Cromwell was anxious to avoid creating a martyr. It was publicly stressed that Sexby had had excellent care and been regularly visited in prison by his wife and his uncle. He had died a natural death and been given a decent funeral.[53]

The fact remains that Edward Sexby died in the Tower, a deranged and obsessed man, after fifteen years of excitement, hope, despair and effort such as he could never have expected when he was apprenticed to the Grocers in 1632. He might then have hoped to become a journeyman, dreamed of becoming a Grocer. He would not, at that time, have imagined playing a part on the national stage, as he, in fact, did. His was not a successful part because victory in the First Civil War was not followed by a just and lasting peace as Sexby and his fellow radicals saw it. The epic struggle which resulted over the years which followed the ending of this war involved treachery and attempted murder, neither of which is to be admired, but men such as Sexby were in a cleft stick. The ideals for which they had fought were betrayed by their own leaders. They themselves were betrayed by their former friends. There can scarcely be a sadder fate than that.

PART 5

Richard Rumbold c.1622–1685

I am sure there was no man marked of God above
another; for no man comes into the world with a saddle
on his back, neither any booted and spurred to ride him.
(Richard Rumbold, 1685)

In his execution speech on 26th June 1685, Richard Rumbold
claimed that he had been fighting against 'these idols of
monarchy and prelacy since he was nineteen years of age,
being now past sixty-three'. It may, therefore, be inferred that
he volunteered at the beginning of the First Civil War in 1642,
before impressment became usual among Roundheads and
Royalists. Like Lockyer, he was a Baptist and, therefore, naturally opposed to the regime of Charles I. He was one of a
small handful of conspirators or rebels in the 1680s who can
be identified among the soldier radicals of the 1640s. As a
trooper in Cromwell's regiment, he officiated at the execution
of Charles I as one of the mounted guards about the scaffold.
Subsequently achieving a commission, he was actively
involved in the Third Civil War.[1]

He first emerged as a radical, a Roundhead soldier with an
interest in what the First Civil War had been about, in March
1649, two months after the King's execution. Disillusionment
with the oligarchy which had seized power set in quite quickly
among soldiers and civilians. A republic had been instituted
with their help but no further concessions to their programme
were forthcoming. Eight troopers from different regiments

147

addressed Fairfax, asserting the soldiers' right to petition which had recently been curtailed by the Council of Officers, and demanding the restoration of the General Council of the Army, including representatives of the rank-and-file, as in 1647. 'Is it not the soldier that endureth the heat and burden of the day, and performeth that work whereof the officers bear the glory and the name?'

Civilian Levellers took up the cause of these troopers, 'the five small Beagles', as they were called, who had hunted the Grandees from Newmarket and Triploe Heath (sites of the two vitally important meetings of the Army in June 1647) to Whitehall. The democratisation of the Army was justified, as previously, by the claim that 'the soldiery may lawfully hold the hands of that general who will turn his cannon against his army on purpose to destroy them, the seamen the hands of that pilot who wilfully runs the ship upon the rock'. The pamphleteer described the treachery of Cromwell and Ireton, the way in which they had let down the soldiers and abandoned their claim to be citizens in arms with the right to petition. 'We were before ruled by King, Lords and Commons; now by a General, Court Martial and Commons'. Five of the men involved were savagely punished – condemned to ride the wooden horse with their faces to the tail and their swords broken over their heads before being cashiered. After their ordeal these five troopers were driven off in coaches and fêted in Leveller pubs by civilian supporters. The other three escaped punishment.[2]*

So many of the soldiers in the New Model Army found politics confusing. They were 'young statesmen'. Richard Rumbold, one of the original eight signatories, explained that he had been 'misled', apologised and therefore escaped punishment. It is easy to imagine a twenty-seven-year-old

---

* 'Riding the wooden horse' was a painful and degrading punishment. Two boards were nailed together so as to make a sharp ridge or angle, with four posts representing the legs of the horse. The rider sat astride, with his hands bound together, for up to an hour, with one or two muskets attached to each leg.

See also p. 132.

trooper being told by his officers that he was endangering his career unnecessarily; that he had, in fact, been deceived by civilians and politicians, that the ruling of the Council of Officers that petitions should be submitted first to regimental officers then to the General and, by him, if he thought fit, to Parliament was the right way to attend to soldiers' grievances. Men should trust their officers: the solidarity of the Army was all-important. Further fighting in Ireland was an immediate prospect – an argument which had proved successful in persuading soldiers to abandon politics in the winter of 1647. Rumbold was thus talked out of his first protest and was rewarded by Cromwell some time later with a commission – not the first time a man had been apparently or temporarily bought off in the New Model Army. The same ploy silenced another signatory, John Breman, one of the soldier-agitators of 1647, commissioned in the 1650s. Neither Rumbold nor Breman* was seduced from the radical cause for long.[3]

Richard Rumbold served throughout the Interregnum as a lieutenant in the cavalry regiment commanded successively by Oliver Cromwell and William Packer, a regiment with a history of political activity in 1647 when Sexby was one of its agitators, but regarded as sufficiently trustworthy in January 1649 for the job of keeping the crowds back from the scaffold on the day of the King's execution. Rumbold fought at Dunbar and at Worcester. He lost an eye and acquired the nickname Hannibal. After the Restoration he was one of nearly three thousand officers recently dismissed or disbanded and seeking employment. He had the luck or skill to marry a widow with a substantial house and a brewing business, which he carried on for her. He was, therefore, a man of some substance, risking his life, family and property in opposition to Charles II and his regime. He hankered after the good old days as well as the Good Old Cause, choosing old comrades from the New Model Army as his friends and allies and longing for leadership. Not surprisingly, his first choice was a contemporary of his own, a gentleman and a soldier, General Edmund Ludlow,

---

*For Breman's future activities see p. 138.

a regicide with a noble fighting reputation in the Civil Wars, currently in exile in Vevey, writing his memoirs and well-aware of the hopelessness of the radical cause in England.[4]

Opposition to Charles II was split into many fragments. There were aristocratic critics of the government: the Earl of Shaftesbury, Lord William Russell, Algernon Sidney and the Earl of Essex, future Whigs,* members of the Green Ribbon Club, established in the 1670s. Green had been the Leveller colour, adopted in deference to Thomas Rainborough's sea-faring background, but this was green of a different shade. Aristocrats were not prepared to co-operate with ordinary men. Thirty years or so had passed since the freedom of speech at Putney in the autumn of 1647 and co-operation between officers and men in the New Model Army. The gentry had learned to fear the rabble, 'the poorest he in England' and his fellows. Of the aristocratic Whigs, only Shaftesbury would have anything to do with the group to which Rumbold belonged.[5]

The opposition was divided in terms of aim as well as terms of social class. James, Duke of York, was feared by all as heir to the throne and a known Roman Catholic. This was danger-ous because it was so obvious that, given the prevailing climate of opinion in England and Scotland, toleration or pref-erence for Roman Catholics could only be achieved by the use of arbitrary power. Charles II was feared by many as a crypto-Roman Catholic, 'worse than the Duke because the more secret', and prone to use the Duke as a screen, as one of Rumbold's friends opined. William of Orange, Protestant champion of the future, was in his twenties, with much on his own plate when the first attempt to exclude James from the succession was made. The opposition of the early 1680s scarcely thought of him, or, if they did, regarded him as a probable supporter of his uncles.

The Duke of Monmouth was not a natural leader, in spite

---

* Originally Whiggamore, a term of abuse, applied to Scots Presbyterian rebels.

of his popular appeal. His attitude to his supposed father, the King, was ambivalent although, in the main, loyal. His bastardy, a 'title not allow'd', would always ensure that he depended on 'the Crowd' or on an astute politician. He seemed to Shaftesbury the best bet, which was the most that could be said for him. A point which regularly exercised the radicals was the possibility that Monmouth would turn on them once the Duke of York and the King had been eliminated. There were very few committed Republicans or apologists for a republic.* The recent republics had scarcely been successful or popular: Oliver Cromwell had been within an ace of adopting the title of King four months before his death.[6]

Opposition may have been fragmented and woefully short of leaders between 1660 and 1688 – it was nonetheless constant and constantly dangerous. Seven insurrections and numerous plots and counter-plots, involving England and Scotland, took place during these twenty-eight years Only between 1672 and 1678 was the atmosphere reasonably quiet and this was because religious toleration, fundamental to the radical cause, was in practice in operation during those years. Throughout Charles II's reign, the government operated a spy service comparable to Cromwell's, employing the same methods and many of the same people and costing almost as much. (The amount spent by Cromwell's government on intelligence was greatly exaggerated in the 1660s.) Informers, spies and stool-pigeons were encouraged and rewarded, double agents abounded and conspirators knew the perils which they faced. Richard Rumbold was so well aware of the temptations of poverty that he gave £100 to an associate in 1683 lest want should lead him to treachery. The payment turned out to be insufficient: the man was 'sinking in his business and began to think that of a witness would be the better trade'.[7]

---

* James Harrington advocated a republic in *Oceana*, published in 1656, but his work could also have been interpreted as a defence of limited monarchy. Henry Nevile, in *Plato Redivivus*, published in 1680, put forward a plea for classical republicanism but this was not practical English politics. Milton and Marvell were literary republicans. There was little chance of the emergence of a serious political programme in the 1680s, and certainly not a popular one, from the works of any of these writers.

The position of the opposition in 1681 was very much weaker than it had been in 1642. Scotland, Ireland and the navy were all under Royal control which had not been the case under Charles I. A standing army of 6,000 men, modelled on the household guards of Louis XIV, was in existence. Charles II and his brother were attended by mounted guards whenever they left London – when they went to Newmarket, for instance. When Parliament was not sitting, prorogued, if not dissolved, criticism was restricted to grumbling – in news-sheets, pamphlets, taverns and clubs. Critics were well aware of their own powerlessness. It is not surprising that violent methods came to be considered. In the words of Shaftesbury: 'Resistance [had to be] envisaged'. John Wildman was the first to suggest the employment of 'some brisk lads' to destroy the King and the Duke of York.[8]

The most famous and notorious of the conspiracies or supposed conspiracies of Charles II's reign was the so-called Popish Plot. In September 1678, Titus Oates told the Privy Council of Catholic plans for risings in England, Scotland and Ireland and a plot to murder the King and bring about the succession of the Duke of York. Oates was a liar but his words fell on willing and credulous ears. He was supported by Israel Tonge, a minister in London of doubtful sanity, convinced that the great fire of 1666 had actually been the work of Catholics. Sir Edmund Berry Godfrey, the magistrate to whom Oates first made his allegation, was found dead in suspicious circumstances within a few weeks of the matter becoming the business of the Privy Council. In the words of a contemporary, Godfrey's murder proved the plot and the plot proved the murder.* Over a period of four years, thirty-five people lost their lives by judicial process which might, more accurately, be described as judicial murder. Two days after the death of

---

*Most recent research suggests that Sir Edmund, in fact, committed suicide and his relations suborned the coroner's jury to bring in a verdict of murder and thus protect the dead man's considerable assets from confiscation by the State.

Charles II in 1685, Oates suffered the most savage punishment possible for perjury.[9]

It is not creditable that, although they had no hand in fabricating the plot, the aristocratic Whigs took up the revelations of Titus Oates and Israel Tonge in 1678 to embarrass the government and break free from the stalemate with which they were faced. Their aim was to achieve the dissolution of the Parliament which had sat since 1661 and been superlatively managed in the Court or government interest, and to obtain a new Parliament which might accurately represent the country's hysterical fear of a Roman Catholic King.

Oates's evidence in front of the Privy Council, on his first appearance, included some information supplied by a 'Mr Rumboll', obtained from a Mr Nevill who lived in Ireland. It seems possible and almost probable that this was Richard Rumbold, whose name was frequently written 'Rumboll' by contemporaries and by himself as his quoted letter shows.* The radicals as well as the aristocratic Whigs were apparently willing to involve themselves in the Popish Plot for their own ends at a very early stage. Frustration produces desperation. After a time, opposition in Charles II's reign could not afford to be scrupulous about either tools or methods.[10]

Constitutional methods were tried between 1679 and 1681. The nation proved to be solidly opposed to James's succession. Three general elections were held within three years, two in 1679 and one in 1681: a Whig House of Commons was always elected and a bill to exclude the Duke of York from the succession was always passed – but blocked by the Lords. The Royal Prerogative to summon, prorogue and dissolve Parliament was used to the best advantage. In October 1679 Parliament only met to be immediately adjourned for one year. It was summoned to meet in Tory Oxford in April 1681, ostensibly because of plague in London and dismissed after one week. Plot hysteria abated with time. Parliament was not necessary financially for Charles II as by 1681 funds were assured

---

* See p. 161.

from Louis XIV and by improved revenue from trade. The Whig cause had been weakened by division between those who supported Exclusion and the succession of the Duke of Monmouth and those who supported the succession of James with considerable limitations of his prerogative. Even without this divide, constitutional methods had no chance of success. Charles II, a consummate politician, was well aware of this. Attending the final debate in the House of Lords, thoughtfully warming himself by the fire, he turned gracefully to the bishops and remarked: 'I have the Church and nothing can ever separate us'. Not even my own treachery, he might have added. James II, much more honourable than his brother in matters of religion, lost his throne when he finally forfeited the support of the Anglican hierarchy.[11]

'Hannibal' Rumbold was recruited in the winter of 1682 or spring of 1683 by a young man called Robert West, a lawyer, too young to have fought in the war, possibly a republican who had contacts among old soldiers, Monmouth supporters in the west country and London recently outraged by Privy Council interference with the government of the City and the imposition of Tory sheriffs and a Tory Lord Mayor.* Rumbold was known to another young lawyer in West's group, one who had lost his job as under-sheriff in the Tory *coup*, named Richard Goodenough. Goodenough had acted for Rumbold in a debt case in March 1682. Rumbold was a particularly valuable recruit, not only because of his character and personality, 'a brisk man of interest', according to a hostile contemporary, but also because of where he lived.

Once legal methods of opposition had failed, the choice lay between rebellion and murder, murder of the Duke of York alone, or of the King and the Duke of York. (Of course, choice also lay between the succession of Monmouth as King and the establishment of a Commonwealth or Republic, but the latter seemed increasingly unfeasible.) Murder was both

---

* Sheriffs were responsible for empanelling juries and could thus protect the accused of their own party. A Whig jury, for example, had secured the acquittal of Shaftesbury in November 1681 when the government was determined to reassert its control and be revenged on those who had supported Exclusion.

cheaper and easier than a co-ordinated rebellion – given government intelligence services and the proliferation of informers. The movements of the King and Duke of York were predictable: the two seldom strayed from a routine path which included two visits every year to the races at Newmarket. Richard Rumbold's house was superbly situated for an ambush when the brothers were returning to London from the races. He said himself that the idea of attacking the King, his brother and his bastard son at this point had been mooted ten years earlier.[12]

A narrow by-road which served as a short cut on the way from Newmarket to London ran from Bishop's Stortford to Hoddesden in Hertfordshire. On one side it was bordered by a thick hedge and ditch; on the other, by Rye House, with a watchtower and gardens, surrounded by a moat, accessible by a single bridge. A range of stables and barns extended from the garden, forming a courtyard in which men and horses could be hidden from the road. London was eighteen miles away; mounted men could travel over Hackney Marsh and arrive in the capital as soon or sooner than the news of a successful attempt, either to take cover or to proceed with the establishing of a new regime. Plans had been made for seizing the Tower.[13]

Meetings were held throughout February and March 1683 to plan the ambush. The chief conspirators were West himself, Colonel John Rumsey, a New Model veteran, and Richard Goodenough. These men invited Robert Ferguson, a Scottish minister, to return from exile in the Netherlands (where he had been for the last three months) and help them. Ferguson, a veritable turncoat and subsequent enthusiastic Jacobite, was, at this time, devoted to Monmouth and prepared to act as an *agent-provocateur* on his behalf, to discover all he could about the plot and circumvent it if possible. Monmouth, himself, was prepared to conspire against the regime but not to countenance the murder of the King. 'You must think of me as a son,' as he said, a remark which (understandably) 'damped the design for some time and always dogged it'. Rumbold was designated leader of the attack. Toasts were drunk to 'Hannibal and his boys', weapons, horses and finance were all discussed and a plan agreed.*[14]

The moral issue raised its head. Rumbold longed for a leader he could trust and asked for General Ludlow to be invited to come back to England. It was impossible to contact him in the time available. (It is, in fact, most unlikely that Ludlow, by now sadly pessimistic about the Good Old Cause, would have accepted. When he was asked to command a rebel force in the west of England in 1684 he refused on the ground that he had 'done his work ... in the World.') Professional soldiers naturally disliked the idea of falling on unarmed men. Rumbold and Thomas Walcott, a former officer in Ludlow's own troop, who was to be one of the attackers, were eventually reconciled to the notion of a military ambush rather than a murderous shooting, a notion easy to maintain by reason of the fact that the King and the Duke of York were habitually accompanied by guards. Walcott stipulated that he would attack the guards but not the King in his coach. West claimed that it was 'never thought injustice to shoot ... wolves and tigers', an argument similar to that used against the Grandees in 1649 and, forty-two years earlier, against Strafford. Rumbold is reported, not very reliably, as concluding that killing the two brothers might prevent rebellion and bloodshed and could thus be interpreted as keeping one of the commandments. He was clearly wrestling with his conscience, and his scruples seem to have been overcome; practically, he claimed to need no less than forty well-armed men. There was need for safety in numbers in view of the danger of reprisals from Monmouth if the attempt were successful. Recruiting these men was entrusted to Robert Ferguson, Richard Goodenough and Rumbold himself, who concentrated their efforts respectively on Scotsmen, Londoners from East Smithfield and Wapping and old soldiers. These recruits were not just hit-men. 'Most persons insisted on terms: religion, liberties and properties. They would not fight "to change persons only but things."'[15]

---

*Evidence concerning the Rye House Plot and the events of 1682–83 is complicated and controversial. It is fully discussed in Appendix B.

The attack was planned for Sunday 1st April, when the King and the Duke were expected to return from Newmarket. Arms were a necessity, to be carried to Rye House in market carts from Smithfield or barges transporting oysters up the river Ware or by the men under their coats. Rumbold required carbines, pistols and swords. One of his tasks was to find a spy to make sure that the two brothers travelled together. His men were to ride to Rye House in pairs the day before, his servants who were not party to the plot were to be sent to the market early in the morning and his wife and daughters to be locked upstairs for safety. Rye House was near the end of a stage: horses and guards would be tired and it would be easy for men posing as farm-workers to block off the far end of the narrow road while others fell on the coach, its guards and its occupants. Everything seemed under way twelve days before the attack, but it was not to be. A careless groom, smoking in a stable in Newmarket, caused what was afterwards described as a 'Providential Fire, defeating a black conspiracy'. The King's house was saved but much damage was done to his coaches and horses and the smoke in the town was insufferable. An immediate plan was made for the royal party to remove to Cambridge and thence to London. This was subsequently cancelled in favour of return by the Rye House route on Monday 26th March.[16]

Communications between the conspirators and Newmarket were excellent. They knew about the fire and the planned movements of the King as soon as the government did. 'We star'd upon one another like baffled Fools', as West said, but they rallied and discussed alternative plans. The weekend of 24th–25th was not long enough for setting up the ambush for Monday. There was a shortage of ready money for the immediate procurement of horses; purchase of the latter in quantity on a Sunday (25th) would arouse suspicion. The notion of killing the King and the Duke on that occasion was regretfully abandoned but the plotting continued, the government nervously aware of it. A notice in the *London Gazette* declared that 'Idle Persons begging for relief, pretending to be undone by the fire at Newmarket, should *not* be given relief in

London, they are failed rebels. No one from Newmarket is abroad and begging'.[17]

Robert West's group continued to meet throughout the next three months. They held meetings in various taverns – it was safer to keep changing the venue – discussing assassination or rebellion or both. Recruiting continued at a house in St Botolph's, Bishopsgate, which belonged to Richard Rumbold's cousin, John Gladman, another veteran of the New Model Army, and was frequented by others of the same ilk: William Rumbold, Richard's brother, Abraham Holmes, a former agitator, agent of the fugitive Earl of Argyll, and Samuel Packer, who had been Richard Goodenough's deputy. As the numbers grew so also did the fear of betrayal. The government was, in any case, alert and suspicious. Information with regard to the movements and occupations of Rumbold and Gladman, among others, came in front of the Secretary of State in April.[18]

West had been able to explain a collection of arms by reason of his plantation in the New World: he needed money to pay for these and Ferguson had promised this. He told West that John Wildman would pay £100 but would only hand that sum over to Richard Rumbold in person. Rumbold went accordingly, by arrangement, to collect it at 5 a.m. one morning, only to be told that Wildman had 'gone out of town'. He complained to West that Wildman was 'unintelligible', blowing hot and cold on the murder plan which had originally been his own idea. He had recently shown Rumbold a paper which he had written, outlining current grievances 'yet keeping within the law.' When West met Wildman on the Exchange and grumbled that things were so bad that he was thinking of emigrating, Wildman had replied fiercely; 'Don't talk of being driven out, drive them out.' Ferguson later explained to Rumbold that Wildman had had a change of heart. The truth of the matter is that the major was always very careful of his own skin, ready for others to take an active part in any driving out there was to be done. After 1688 he was rewarded with

158

lucrative office and, in 1692, with a knighthood, eventually dying in his bed, having seen two generations of his accomplices die on the gallows.*[19]

The West group was betrayed in June 1683 by Josiah Keeling and his brother, John, who sent a warning to Richard Goodenough. Keeling had been one of the plotters responsible for Wapping; he was known to be in debt and Rumbold had given him £100 to ensure his loyalty. Rumbold had also told West that if he was sure of Keeling's treachery he would have no hesitation in killing him but that he could not risk killing an innocent man. On receiving the warning, seven of the leaders met at West's lodging and decided on flight. At first they planned to hire a ship and go together but this was too dangerous; it became a case of each man for himself. The wily Ferguson comforted the others: 'Gentlemen you are strangers to this kind of exercise, I have been used to fly, I will never be out of a plot so long as I live, and yet hope to meet some of you at Dunbar before Michaelmas.' Rumbold got safely to the Netherlands. By 23rd June there was a price of £100 on his head. On that same day Robert West turned King's Evidence, followed by John Rumsey. These two were the chief witnesses in the trials of greater and lesser plotters which occupied the next four weeks.[20]

Four men were executed in London during July 1683, one was acquitted and one committed suicide, or, more probably, was murdered when he was in prison, awaiting trial. Other executions followed within the next few months. A frantic search for papers and for concealed weapons took place. Informers were questioned many times. Suspected Scotsmen were sent to Edinburgh for trial because torture could be legally used north of the border. From the Netherlands on 2nd August, Rumbold wrote West the following letter:

Sir
When I consider what misery has fallen on our party by your evidence I cannot think of you but with amazement

---

*For other evidence of Wildman's character see p. 141.

and horror as if you were born for the subversion of your country and ruin of the Protestant religion. But when I reflect on your behaviour and consider with what subtlety and artifice our enemies deluded you and when I [understand] with what reluctance you were induced to accuse those men you had solicited, stirred up and trusted to so high a degree I cannot but have charity for your frailty and compassion for your sufferings... When I further observe how you [confused] our enemies by deluding them with hearsay information and halloeing them upon Hone, Rouse and Walcot and, in the meanwhile, by the faithful concealing of some and the late naming of others you have given a great many brave men not only a warning but opportunity to escape the grip of popish cruelty. For my part I cannot sufficiently admire your conduct neither can I believe that any other person could have saved himself and so many other worthy men in such a general calamity with the loss of only three, two whereof were those most inconsiderable of our party. Hone and Walcott may more justly charge their murders on Percival the Attorney and Shepherd the merchant than you who were compelled to do as you did by invincible necessity whereof your kindness to Captain Blague is clear demonstration but they were villains untold and upon choice. As for the murder of my lord Russell, the blood of that incomparable person cries for vengeance against Shepherd, Howard and that villain, Rumsey who I am convinced hath been the Duke of York's spy and trepan, managed by the Duke of Beaufort ever since he was the Lord's *privado*.* One that had not been wrackbrained might have long since perceived it had he been in that Lord's station. Upon the consideration of all these things I must entreat you not to abandon yourself to oppressive sorrow for next to the mercy of God the charity of your party is not to be despaired of, it is not unknown to any of us with what zeal and sincerity you led us whilst there

---

* *Privado*, a Spanish term, signifying an adviser to an aristocratic patron.

was any hope of succeeding and I shall never cease to represent you to our friends according to your merits. Now you have put yourself out of the reach of your enemies by obtaining a pardon I shall make it my sole business to set you right with your friends which is the least I can do to you to whom I owe my life for had not your wisdom directed me Mr Keeling's villainy had destroyed me. These things, Dear Sir, are never to be forgotten. My service to the best of women your wife and to the worthy man Mr Cox. May he be as happy in those pretty babes his grandchildren as we have been and again may you be notwithstanding those misfortunes with which you are surrounded. I received your letters for me at the place you have lately chose and they will be safely destroyed.

I am hastely yours Ri. Rumball.

Rumbold thus praised West for 'halloeing' – that is, cheering his enemies on – after three men in order to let others escape. William Hone, a London joiner recruited by Goodenough, and John Rouse, a gentleman's servant who had been implicated in the Popish Plot and was much trusted by the Whigs, were the two 'inconsiderables', scapegoats for others. Thomas Walcott would have been sadly missed as an old comrade and worthy soldier. The attorney, Percival, and merchant, Thomas Shepherd, actually played no part in Walcott's trial but 'that villain Rumsey' did. Shepherd, Lord Howard of Escrick and Rumsey were chief witnesses at Lord Russell's trial when West's evidence was rejected as hearsay. William Blague, a sea-captain, was acquitted after standing trial because firm testimony against him from two witnesses was not forthcoming.

In this remarkable letter can be found the shock of betrayal, the guilt of survival, an honest attempt to understand another man's temptation and sympathise with his predicament. Most astonishing of all in these circumstances is the continuing reverence of a follower for a leader. Robert West, a civilian in his twenties, had enlisted and inspired a group of soldiers and civilians, many of them older and more experienced than himself, and welded them into an active force with weapons, finance and plans. He had gaped, and seen his friends gaping, when the King and the Duke of York were saved from the assassination attempt on their way back from the races. He had convened more meetings and considered different plans after the failure of this one. Once betrayal was known, he had invited his associates to his lodging to arrange flight. Then he had turned informer. Rumbold's generosity, sympathy and loyalty to a fallen leader leap from the page. They tell much about his character. It is to be hoped that his letter gave the comfort it was intended to give and that Rumbold was successful in persuading the rest of the party towards the same forgiveness.[21]

There were many men in England who disliked the government of Charles II; in Scotland there were even more who hated it. The Scottish Parliament and the Scottish legal system were restored in 1660 but no kind of Scottish independence. Charles II was actually so secure in England that he could do what his father had failed to do: impose an Episcopal church on Scotland, a church regarded by most Scots as foreign and superstitious. Leading Scotsmen were torn between delight that the Stuart dynasty had been restored and disgust at the loss of true independence for Scotland and the government which kept order among the Covenanters. Lauderdale's government was harsh and tyrannical, provoking the rebellion of 1678, which culminated in the defeat of the rebels at the hands of Monmouth at the battle of Bothwell Bridge. The Duke of York succeeded Lauderdale in 1682 – in Scotland he could not so easily be used as a focus for English anti-Catholicism yet he was well-placed for claiming the succession should his brother's health fail – and proved more hated as well as, apparently, more powerful. He was determined either to make a friend of the most powerful of the Scots nobles, Archibald Campbell, Earl of Argyll, with a huge clan behind him, lord of many acres, or to break him. Argyll's father had been executed in 1661 and Argyll himself, the ninth Earl, condemned to death for verbal treason but reprieved. For twenty-odd years Argyll was content with what he later called 'criminal moderation: he supported Lauderdale, a connection of his by marriage, and fought at the head of his own men at Bothwell Bridge on the government's side. In 1682 he agreed to support the Duke of York in all matters except religion and was then found guilty of treason for qualifying his oath of obedience. He escaped from Edinburgh Castle in November 1682 through the agency of his step-daughter and took refuge in London, sheltered by an old agitator of the New Model and using the alias 'Mr Hope'. At the end of the year he took refuge in the Netherlands, along with many English refugees including the Earl of Shaftesbury.[22]

English and Scottish exiles in Amsterdam, including Monmouth, Argyll and Rumbold, among others, met and plotted an invasion. For Monmouth the situation had clarified with the death of his father and succession of his uncle in February 1685. Monmouth no longer had to think of himself as a son. Argyll was now in command of funds, weapons and an expeditionary force. He planned to lead a rebellion in Scotland, supported, when he arrived, by his clan and by the Presbyterian clergy. A diversion in the south would be an advantage and Monmouth was pushed into agreeing to this as a point of honour. The Scots force of three hundred men and three ships had to sail by the beginning of May; its presence and intentions could not be concealed in Amsterdam for long. Monmouth was left with only one month to organise the supposedly complementary invasion of England.[23]

Two Scotsmen, Andrew Fletcher and Robert Ferguson (acting as chaplain), were to sail with Monmouth. Two Englishmen, John Ayloffe, a New Model veteran and a survivor of the Rye House plot, and Richard Rumbold himself, sailed with Argyll. Rumbold had the rank of colonel and was to command the cavalry expected to materialise when the expedition landed in the Western Highlands. Argyll proved to be a hopeless commander in the field, dallying in his tribal heartlands rather than pressing on into Ayrshire, where many supporters might have been expected. He found himself surrounded by English troops on three sides and was captured in Renfrewshire on 18th June. Ayloffe and Rumbold, who had been wounded, were taken a few days later. Monmouth landed at Lyme Regis on 11th June, only one week before the rebellion in Scotland was crushed.[24]

Rumbold was brought to trial, so-called, on 26th June in Edinburgh 'fettered and bareheaded with a rope round his neck'. Proceedings were hurried up lest he should die of his wounds. His mind was firm and constancy unshaken. He made no objection to the jury and freely confessed his association with Argyll and everything else in the charge except the accusation that he had designed the King's death. He asked all present to believe the words of a dying man when he denied this, he abhorred the very thought of it. He said that he thought kingly government was the best of all, *justly executed*,* i.e. by a King and a legal, freely chosen parliament. According to the law of God, the law of Nations and the law of reason there exists a contract between the King and his subjects; if one party breaks this contract the other party is absolved from it. He therefore took up arms in defence of the just rights of the people against Popery and slavery... At this point in his speech they beat the drums in order to render it inaudible, but his confession of faith was heard:

I die in the faith that God will speedily arise for the deliverance of his church and people. I am sure there was no man marked of God above another; for no man comes into the world with a saddle on his back, neither any booted and spurred to ride him ... not but that I am well satisfied that God hath wisely ordered different stations of men in the world, as I have already said: Kings having as much power as to make them great, and people as much property as to make them happy. And to conclude,

---

* Italics mine.

I shall only add my wishes for the salvation of all men who were created for that end.

He refused the assistance of priests on the scaffold, asking them to express their good wishes for him in their own closets. He wanted to be left to seek God in his own way. Like Montrose before him, he asserted defiantly that he wished he had a limb for every town in Christendom. 'Seeing the Lord is pleased in this manner to take me to himself, I confess, something hard to flesh and blood, yet blessed be his name.'[25]

It is difficult to reconcile Rumbold's dying speech with his reported actions in the autumn of 1682 and spring of 1683. The very choice of Rye House, which Rumbold owned, as the setting for an attack on the King and the Duke of York, quite apart from the testimony of others, involved him in this attack. Contemporaries distinguished between a military ambush, even one in which the attackers greatly outnumbered the prey, and murder. This distinction was made by Walcot at his trial in 1683 and was to be made later by supporters of James II, justifying an attack on William III. Rumbold was prepared to be judged as a soldier, by the rules which govern soldiers in a time of war or, perhaps, old soldiers living under a tyrannical regime supported by a spy service and a standing army. It seems a more likely explanation of his dying speech than that put forward by Robert Ferguson in 1686 that Rumbold had been persuaded by Wildman of the folly of the Rye House plot and 'only pretended to carry on with it'. Such deceit and duplicity does not square with other evidence of Rumbold's character and many contemporary estimates of him.[26]

In many ways Richard Rumbold was an archetypal soldier of the New Model Army: brave, disciplined, Godfearing and thoughtful. His formative years were spent in this remarkable institution, his loyalty to it and to what he thought it had been fighting for remained constant. In the Army, *this* army, he learned to argue in terms of the law of God, the law of reason and the law of Nations. He maintained that a contract existed between the King and his subjects, a contract which could be broken, and had been, by Charles I and his sons. As he said, he was not a republican. It is possible to imagine him hoping for peace and justice after the Restoration and a chance to beat his sword into a ploughshare, to make an honest living for his wife and family. The restored government disgusted him and action seemed to be dictated. He was rewarded by the traditional punishment of traitors. His head and quarters were displayed in Edinburgh, taken down in 1689 when the Whigs triumphed even if the radicals did not. Most of the things for which the radicals had fought so valiantly were secured within the next two hundred years; their contemporary fate was such as might have been expected by soldiers employed on a forlorn hope.

EPILOGUE

No man that warreth entangleth himself with the affairs of this life; that he may please him who hath chosen him to be a soldier. II Timothy 2 v.4. (Authorized Version)

A soldier on active service will not let himself be involved in civilian affairs; he must be wholly at his commanding officer's disposal. II Timothy 2 v.4. (New English Bible)

The *Soldier's Pocket Bible* was first published in 1643. This was a small octavo, fifteen pages of selected texts which might be hoped to inspire and comfort fighting men, taken from the Genevan version of the Scriptures. It was re-published in 1693, by which time British soldiers were fighting a foreign enemy, with a new title: *The Christian Soldier's Penny Bible* and some significant alterations. Texts had been added on the first two pages and half of the last page under the following headings:

I. The Christian soldier's chief aim should be to do his King and Country service, in procuring or preserving the peace of it.

II. The soldier should observe the command of the Lord of Hosts, and acknowledge his authority in obeying his superior.

XX. The Christian soldier should so manage his temporal

warfare (for King and Country) that he may succeed well in his spiritual warfare, and enjoy peace with God eternally.

The duty of obedience and loyalty to King and country is emphatically spelt out. There was to be no place for agitators in future British armies. Superior officers were to be obeyed without question, their authority corresponding to that of the Lord of Hosts. Biblical quotations in the 1693 *Soldier's Bible* were taken from the Authorized Version which differs from the Genevan in its attitude to authority. King James I, who authorised the new translation in 1612, had condemned the Genevan version and its notes as seditious in many places. The last edition of this latter translation came out in 1644.[1]

In 1689, the Declaration of Rights condemned standing armies in time of peace as illegal, making law out of the complaints of the last twenty years. This ban was not maintained: the British army has a continuous history, going back to the reign of Charles II. Soldiers when they enlist are required to swear an oath of allegiance to the monarch. Officers are not: their commission directly and specifically entrusts them with the monarch's business. To lose this commission, in any circumstances, involves not only disgrace and dishonour but also social death. The tradition of loyalty to the monarch and to the State in the British army in the last three centuries has been magnificent. Since the reign of James II the army has never been involved in politics or used to maintain order among civilians. It is a professional force, supplemented, at times, by conscripts who are trained to adapt to existing standards. The New Model, despite its professionalism in the field, represents, in one respect, a stark contrast to the armies which followed it in British history. Exceptional circumstances drove Thomas and William Rainborough, Robert Lockyer, Edward Sexby and Richard Rumbold to volunteer as soldiers. Without the civil wars, it may be supposed that Thomas Rainborough would have been a sea captain and Member of Parliament, like his father, William Rainborough would have made his life in New England, Edward Sexby would have been a Grocer,

168

Robert Lockyer and Richard Rumbold would have followed useful and profitable trades. The most famous member of the New Model, Oliver Cromwell, would have remained a country gentleman. All these men could claim to be citizen soldiers, not mercenaries, men who were fighting for a cause, or rather – and this was where the trouble began as it turned out, different causes.

Cromwell is greatly to be congratulated for preserving such a degree of unity in the Army. Chaos might have resulted if the Army had split at any time during the Interregnum. Those who opposed him, outspokenly and consistently, in the New Model were a tiny minority, a handful of men whose principles are very much more attractive than those of the Grandees but whose hope of success was negligible. 'If only' is a phrase to be deplored but it is tempting to wonder what might have happened if William Rainborough and Edward Sexby had supported Thomas at Ware or if Thomas had not been killed, with the connivance, it seems, of some of his own side, in 1648. Sexby, in that case, might have been clearer in his mind from the moment when the execution of the King was followed by the setting-up of an oligarchy, Rumbold would not have lacked a leader in the 1680s. Thomas Rainborough, unarmed, was killed by armed men. There is no evidence that, when they set off, his killers suffered from the problems of conscience evinced by the Rye House plotters in 1683. A forlorn hope is usually doomed if its leader is picked off.

Leading civilian radicals gave way to disillusion and despair in the second half of the seventeenth century. Furious and argumentative John Lilburne became a Quaker (and the Quakers became pacifists); gentle, scrupulous William Walwyn retired into private life and the practice of medicine; former actor and playwright, most entertaining of pamphleteers, Richard Overton disappeared more completely into private life or hiding; John Wildman, by contrast, did well out of the Glorious Revolution and died in his bed, a rich man with a knighthood, in 1693.

Radical ideas survived and triumphed. This is how the soldier radicals of the seventeenth century are vindicated.

APPENDIX A

Professor Alan Young has attributed Colonel Rainborough's flag to Captain William Rainborough, brother of Colonel Thomas, and William Rainborough's flag to a different William, son rather than brother of the Colonel. It is true that Colonel Rainborough did have a son called William, born between 1639 and 1642, and this son did serve in the Protectorate army, before emigrating to New England after the Restoration. He would not have been old enough to serve in Ireland in 1649 in the campaign for which the severed-head banner was intended.[1]

Three principal sources relate to the Rainborough banners: a work first translated from French in 1646, reprinted in 1648 and 1650, the Turmile collection in Dr Williams's Library and the Sloane manuscripts in the British Library. The French treatise on emblems, their history and significance, was written by Henry Estienne and translated by Thomas Blount under the title *The Making of Devises*. Blount added 'a Catalogue of Coronet Devises on the Parliament's part in the late War', and this includes the following entry: 'Col Rainsborow figured a Bible, inscribed *Verbum Dei*, with a Hand and a flaming sword over it, and the Motto, *Vincit Veritas*', the same description is to be found in the 1650 edition which followed.[2]

Jonathan Turmile collected 'Colours, or Standards and armorial bearings of certain officers in the parliament army 1642 and a list of the colours taken by the earl of Essex ... at Edgehill and also of the colours taken by Sir Thomas Fairfax at Knaseby'. Certain colours intended for the Irish expedition of 1649 were also included. The research into these colours was meticulous: Turmile noted those which 'were intended to be filled in ... but these colours could never be got to be drawn'. Page 79 is blank, marked 'Ransboro'. The severed-head banner is to be found on page 115, 'Maiger Ransbrowe' written below, with the comment 'Col Rainsborow figured a Bible, inscribed *Verbum Dei*, with a hand and flaming sword over it, and the motto, *Vincit Veritas*', exactly the same description as is to be found in Blount.[3] (See Fig. 4)

Confusion has arisen because the artist who drew and painted the colours in the collection preserved by Sir Hans Sloane, president of the Royal Society in succession to Newton in 1727, was not always accurate about rank. Colonel Rainborough's standard is entitled 'Captain Rannsbrowe'. John Lambert is described as Captain with the word 'Colonel' added in the margin. Henry Ireton is described as Captain with no reference to his subsequent promotion. Thomas Ayloffe, Colonel of a foot regiment in Manchester's army, is also described as Captain. It is fortunate that the drawing of the Bible, mailed fist, flaming sword and two mottoes exists, illustrating precisely Colonel Rainborough's standard as described by Blount and Turmile. The Saracen's head, drawn below, is typical of an infantry colonel who tended to use his family badge on his colour if he was not armigerous.[4]

APPENDIX B

The Rye House Plot

Of the Rye house Plot it may be said much more truly than of the Popish, that there was in it some truth mixed with much falsehood. (Charles James Fox 1808)

'All was but talk' – with the gloss 'all plots begin with talk'. (Bishop Burnet 1705, with Dean Swift's comment)

Scepticism about the Rye House Plot in particular and the plotting which is alleged to have taken place throughout the period 1682–85 was initially contemporary. Even as investigations were going on, men remembered the lies and deceptions of the Popish Plot and the shameful betrayal of justice. It continued among historians, especially those with a motive for whitewashing their own party. In the eighteenth century, history was written with a purpose – the justification of specific political principles. Whig historians like Fox and Macaulay had to refute Tory historians like Hume. There was no such thing as impartial history. After 1689, in the wake of their Glorious, bloodless and aristocratic Revolution, the Whigs and their historians were seriously concerned to extol their heroes, Russell and Sydney, and also to whitewash their past, to distance themselves from illegal and treasonable activities and low-class radical allies. The evidence for these activities and these associations was sufficiently unsatisfactory for disavowal to be easy and believable. At the same time it was possible to affirm that the spurious evidence of informers had been used to bring down great men feared by the government.[1]

Most of the evidence for the Rye House Plot itself and for the plotting which occupied the period 1682–84 comes from informers, speaking for their lives, concerned, above all, to escape prosecution themselves. There are, however, such a number of these that their stories can be compared and contrasted with each other and some measure of truth or probability secured. Josiah Keeling, Robert West, John Rumsey and Lord Howard of Escrick confessed freely in the early stages of discovery. Lord Grey, Nathaniel Wade and James Holloway confessed after capture, William Carstares, after capture and torture. Lord Russell, John Hampden, Thomas Walcott, Thomas Armstrong and Algernon Sydney all stood trial. Monmouth was pardoned for his share in the plotting of 1682–83 after confession to his father. Robert Ferguson wrote his account of Rye House in 1686 when he was living in Amsterdam, with the assistance of John Wildman, also in exile there at that time.

The trials of Lord Russell and Algernon Sydney certainly reflect no credit on the government of Charles II. Despite his plea of innocence, Russell may have been guilty of misprision of treason. He admitted that he had heard 'many things and said some things contrary to my duty' and his papers were almost certainly burnt, but the verdict and sentence at his trial were procured by the timely disclosure of Essex's supposed suicide in prison. The witness, Lord Howard, asked pardon dramatically for his broken voice: 'I was just now acquainted with the fate of my lord of Essex.' Judge Jeffreys rammed the point home in his summing up: Essex was 'guilty of such desperate things ... [that he killed himself] to avoid public justice'. The jury in Russell's case was thus shockingly manipulated, convinced of widespread treason and aristocratic involvement in this. (The affair appears yet more disgraceful in view of the probability that Essex was actually murdered in prison and suicide evidence faked by minions of the Duke of York, acting on his orders.) When Sydney, who denied any involvement in plotting at all, was tried in November, the state could only find one man, Lord Howard of Escrick, to testify against him. Two witnesses were required in treason trials, so the prosecution hit on the idea of using his own writings as evidence against the accused man who was thus, in effect, condemned out of his own mouth. His final statement to the world, issued in lieu of an execution speech which could be drowned by drums or misreported, defiantly affirmed that his enemies condemned him in order to establish the reality of treasonable designs they claimed to have discovered.[2]

These trials were corrupt but it was true that from the moment when the Oxford Parliament was dissolved, the government of the City of London secured in Tory hands by means of rigged elections, and two illnesses of the King heightened alarm at the prospect of his brother's accession, conspirators discussed the possibilities of rebellion and murder. Throughout this time the same names crop up again and again. Some died in 1683, some lived to fight and die in 1685, a few survived to take part in William's invasion – 'some loyal Rye House and Sedgemore men, true disciples of honest old Rumbold and Robin Ferguson', according to prints of the day.[3]

The ambush at Rye House was seriously planned. It may not have been certain of success even without the fire. At Walcot's trial West explained, 'the thing could not have been effected if the fire had not happened'; the conspirators lacked horses and were not really ready. West was trying to help Walcot, but men should be judged by their intentions rather than their failure to carry these out. Rumbold's letter of 2nd August testifies to West's organisation and the involvement of a party led by West. The government announcement that beggars, supposedly ruined by the Newmarket fire, were actually failed rebels, shows that it was under no illusion. Among many names of observed persons whose movements and activities were reported to the Secretary of State are those of Rumbold and his cousin, Gladman, in the month after the fire, two months before Keeling's disclosure. The plot was real. Many escaped to the Netherlands; radical Wapping proved an excellent port for refugees. In the Low Countries they would find friends and leaders and the chance to try their luck again against the evil of arbitrary government.[4]

PRINCIPAL EVENTS MENTIONED IN THE TEXT		THOMAS RAINBOROUGH BORN c.1610
1629–1640	Personal Rule of Charles I	1639 Married
April 1640	Short Parliament	
Nov. 1640 –1649	Long Parliament	
Sept. 1641	Commons Resolutions concerning Church practices	
Oct 1641	Irish Rebellion	
Jan. 1642	Arrest of the Five Members Charles I left London	Death of father, Captain William Rainborough, MP
April 1842	Charles I refused entry to Hull	
June 1642	Parliamentary Ordinance for men, money etc. King's Commissions of Array	
July 1642	Adventurers' expedition to Ireland First blood shed in the Civil War Navy secured by Parliament	Invested in the Irish Adventure Sailed with the expedition
Aug 1642	King's Standard erected	
Oct 1642	Battle of Edgehill	
June 1643	The Cessation (suspension of hostilities in Ireland)	
Sept 1643	Solemn League and Covenant between Parliament and the Scots	
Oct 1643	Hull engagement	Entered land service with the rank of colonel. Taken prisoner and exchanged
July 1644	Battle of Marston Moor	Served in the army of the
Nov 1644–	Peace negotiations later known as	Eastern Association
Feb 1645	Treaty of Uxbridge	Capture of Crowland Dec 1644
Feb 1645	Self Denying Ordinance	Colonel of Foot in the New Model Army
June 1645	Battle of Naseby	Fought at Naseby Commanded sieges of
Aug 1645	Writs for Recruiter MPs issued	Nunney Castle
Sept 1645		Berkeley Castle
April 1646		Woodstock
–July 1646		Worcester Played important part in siege of Bristol and siege of Corfe Castle Elected Recruiter MP for Droitwich in Worcestershire

ROBERT LOCKYER	WILLIAM RAINBOROUGH	EDWARD SEXBY	RICHARD RUMBOLD
BORN c.1626	BORN c.1612	BORN c.1616	BORN c.1622
	1639 Emigrated to New England	1632 Apprenticed to the Grocers' Company	
	Death of father Captain William Rainborough, MP		
Adult Baptism Volunteered for Parliament	Returned to England Married Invested in the Irish Adventure Sailed with the expedition		Volunteered for Parliament
		Enlisted in Cromwell's troop, the Ironsides 1643	
	Took part in Essex's Cornish campaign as captain in Colonel Sheffield's regiment of horse		
Trooper in Whalley's regiment of horse in the New Model Army	Captain in Sheffield's regiment of horse in the New Model Army	Trooper in Fairfax's regiment of horse in the New Model Army	Trooper in the New Model Army. Regiment unknown
Fought at Naseby	Fought at Naseby	Fought at Naseby	
	Involved in south-west campaign including the siege of Bristol		

	PRINCIPAL EVENTS MENTIONED IN THE TEXT	THOMAS RAINBOROUGH
May 1646	Charles I surrendered to the Scots	
March 1647	Parliament plans to disband the New Model Army	
	Soldiers' Apologie and petition of officers and soldiers	
	Large Petition of the civilian Levellers	
	Declaration of Dislike	
April 1647	Appointment of Agitators	
March–May 1647	Saffron Walden meetings at Headquarters with Parliamentary Commissioners	Plan for expedition to Jersey
June 1647	Seizure of siege train in Oxford	Regiment involved
	Seizure of King at Holmby	
	Newmarket meeting and Solemn Engagement of the Army	
	General Council of the Army called into being	
	Triploe Heath meeting and Declaration of the Army	Colonel Rainborough and his
July 1647	Reading debates	regiment present
	Heads of Proposals	
Aug 1647	London entered by the New Model Army	Colonel Rainborough in
Sept 1647	New Agents appointed	command of 4 regiments
	Case of the Army. First Agreement of the People	which entered Southwark
Oct–Nov 1647	Putney Debates	Leading speaker at Putney
Nov 1647	Escape of the King from Hampton Court	
	Ware Mutiny	Colonel Rainborough present at Ware
Dec 1647	Engagement between the King and the Scots	
	Christmas Day riot at Canterbury	
Jan 1648		Took up his command as Vice-Admiral of the Fleet
April 1648	Army Prayer meeting	
	Outbreak of the Second Civil War	
May 1648	The Deal incident involving the impostor Cornelius Evans	Returned to London
	Naval mutiny	
	Rising in Kent	
June–Aug 1648	Siege of Colchester	Colonel of the Tower Guard,
	Battle of Preston	engaged in the siege
Aug 1648	Execution of Sir Charles Lucas and Sir George Lisle	
Sept 1648	The petition of 11 September	
Oct 1648	Siege of Pontefract	Murder, 29th October 1648
Nov 1648	The Whitehall Debates	
Dec 1648	Pride's Purge	
	Rump of Long Parliament left sitting	

ROBERT LOCKYER BORN c.1626	WILLIAM RAINBOROUGH BORN c.1612	EDWARD SEXBY BORN c.1616	RICHARD RUMBOLD BORN c.1622
	Officer-agitator for his regiment At Saffron Walden meetings	Instigated appointment of Agitators Mar–April 1647 Examined by the Commons in connection with the soldiers' petition April 1647	
	Promoted major. Regiment now commanded by Thomas Harrison		
	Speaker at Putney	Speaker at Putney	
Present at Ware apart from regiment			
		Took no part in the fighting of the Second Civil war associated with Leveller leaders in London	
Regiment involved in the siege of Colchester	Fought at Preston	Carried a letter from John Lilburne to Cromwell and the news of Preston from Oliver Cromwell to the Commons	

PRINCIPAL EVENTS MENTIONED
IN THE TEXT

THOMAS
RAINBOROUGH
BORN c.1610

Jan 1649	2nd Agreement of the People
	Trial and execution of King Charles I
	Commonwealth set up
Feb 1649	Publication of *England's New Chains Discovered*
March 1649	8 Troopers petition Fairfax for the re-establishment
	of the General Council of the Army including
	Agitators
	Publication of *The Hunting of the Foxes*
Apr 1649	Mutiny in London
May 1649	Mutiny quelled at Burford
	The Third Civil War
1649–50	Campaign in Ireland
1650	Campaign in Scotland
Sept 1650	Battle of Dunbar
Sept 1651	Battle of Worcester
May 1650	Adultery Act
Aug 1650	Blasphemy Act
	A Single Eye All Light, No Darkness published
April 1653	Rump of Long Parliament dismissed
Jul–Dec	Barebones or Nominated Parliament
1653	
Dec 1653	Protectorate established
May 1657	The Major Generals, *Killing No Murder* published
Sept 1658	Death of Oliver Cromwell
Sept 1658–	
May 1659	Protectorate of Richard Cromwell
	New Commonwealth
Feb 1660	Monck's march South
Apr 1660	The Convention
May 1660	The Restoration
Dec 1660	Overton's Plot
Oct 1678	The Popish plot and murder of Sir Edward
	Berry Godfrey
1679–	Exclusion crisis
1681	
1683	Rye House Plot
Feb 1685	Death of Charles II
June 1685	Argyll and Monmouth invasions
Dec 1688	Glorious Revolution

ROBERT LOCKYER BORN c.1626	WILLIAM RAINBOROUGH BORN c.1612	EDWARD SEXBY BORN c.1616	RICHARD RUMBOLD BORN c.1622
			A guard of the scaffold at the King's execution
		Appointed by the Commonwealth government to arrest the Scottish Commissioners.	One of the original 8 petitioners, repented and escaped punishment
Executed 27/4/49	Prepared for service in Ireland. 2 Troops in his regiment mutinied without their officers Dismissed from New Model Army 1649	Commissioned with rank of captain and appointed Governor of Portland	Given a commission
	A Ranter and supporter of L. Clarkson in 1650s 1650 Proposed for naval service	Promoted Lt-Colonel sent to Scotland and besieged Tantallon Castle Court-martialled June 1651 Diplomatic mission in France Oct 1651–	
	Feb 1653 Requested naval service for himself	Aug 1653 Engaged in plotting against the Protector and escaped to the Netherlands Secret visit to England to plan murder of Oliver Cromwell, 1656	1651–59 Served as lieutenant in the cavalry regiment of Cromwell and Packer
	Appointed Militia Commissioner and then Colonel of the Horse for combined militias of 3 counties Arrested December Emigrated to New England c. 1661	Captured in England July 1657 Death in prison Jan 1658	Married c. 1661, a maltster at Rye House Hoddesden Involved in Popish Plot. 1682–83 involved in Rye House Plot June 1683 Escaped to the Netherlands May–June 1685 Involved in Argyll's invasion of Scotland 26th June 1685 executed

181

ABBREVIATIONS

Place of publication London, if not otherwise stated.

Abbott: Wilbur Cortez Abbott: *The Writings and Speeches of Oliver Cromwell* (4 vols.) OUP edtn, 1988.

Ashley: Maurice Ashley: *John Wildman, Plotter and Postmaster*, 1947.

Aubrey: ed. Oliver Lawson Dick: *Aubrey's Brief Lives*, Penguin edtn, 1972.

Capp: B.S. Capp: *Cromwell's Navy*, OUP, 1989.

Clarendon: *The History of the Rebellion and Civil Wars in England* (6 vols.), OUP, 1958, 1969.

Clarke: *The Clarke Papers* (ed. C.H. Firth), Vols. I and II, new preface Austin Woolrych (1992), Vols, III and IV, Camden Society, 1891–1901.

Firth and Davies: C.H. Firth and G. Davies: *The Regimental History of Cromwell's Army* (2 vols.), 1940.

Gardiner, History: S.R. Gardiner: *History of England 1603–1642* (10 vols.), 1893.

Gardiner, HCW: S.R. Gardiner: *History of the Great Civil War* (4 vols.), 1901.

Gardiner, HCP: S.R. Gardiner: *History of the Commonwealth and Protectorate* (3 vols.), 1903.

Gentles: Ian Gentles: *The New Model Army in England, Ireland and Scotland, 1645–1653*, Blackwell, Oxford, 1992.

Maseres: Francis Baron Maseres: *Select Tracts Relating to the Civil Wars in England* (2 vols.), 1815.

Morton: Freedom: A.L. Morton: *Freedom in Arms*, 1975.

Morton: Ranters: A.L. Morton: *The World of the Ranters*.

Nicholas: ed. George Warner: *The Nicholas Papers* (4 vols.), Camden Society, 1886.

Rushworth: *The Historical Collections of John Rushworth* (8 vols.) 1680–1701.

Sprigge: Joshua Sprigge: *Anglia Rediviva*, England's Recovery (1647).

State Trials: *Cobbett's Complete Collection of State Trials* (34 vols.), 1809–28.

Thomason Tracts in the British Library E references and 669.

Thurloe: ed. T. Birch: *A Collection of State Papers of John Thurloe* (7 vols.), 1742.

Woodhouse: ed. A.S.P. Woodhouse: *Puritanism and Liberty*, 1950.

Woolrych: Austin Woolrych: *Soldiers and Statesmen: The General Council of the Army and its Debates 1647–1648*, OUP, 1987.

Wootton: ed. David Wootton: *Divine Right and Democracy*, Penguin, 1986.

C.J.: Commons' Journals.

E.H.R.: *English Historical Review*.

L.J.: Lords' Journals.

C.S.P.D.: *Calendar of State Papers Domestic*.

Radicals' Dict: R.L. Greaves and R. Zaller (eds.): *Biographical Dictionary of British Radicals in the Seventeenth Century* (3 vols.), 1982–84.

184

REFERENCES

Introduction

1. Gardiner HCP Vol. III p.93.
2. Monck: quoted G. Davies: *The Early Stuarts* (OUP, 1959) p. 250; Waller quoted C.R. Markham: *Life of Fairfax* (1870) p. 53; Sexby: *Killing No Murder* in Wootton: p. 375.
3. Pepys *Diary* (Everyman edtn) Vol. I p. 452.
4. *A Representation of the Army* 14th June 1647 in Woodhouse p. 404.
5. ed. John Dunn: *Democracy: The Unfinished Journey*, chapter V 'The Levellers': David Wootton p. 71 (OUP 1992).
6. *A Declaration of some Proceedings of John Lilburne* 14. Feb 1648 in *The Leveller Tracts 1647–1653* ed. W. Haller and G. Davies (Columbia UP 1944) pp. 90–134.
7. P. Zagorin: *The Court and the Country* (1969) p. 23; William Shakespeare: *Julius Caesar* Act I Sc. 1, *Henrv V* Act IV Sc. 8; Clarendon Vol. III p. 437.
8. Michael Neill: *Issues of Death* (OUP 1997) pp. 267, 272, 280 and 286.
9. J.A. Sharpe: *Crime in Early Modern England* (1984) p. 24; Brian Manning: *The English People and The English Revolution* (Penguin edtn. 1979) pp. 147–8.
10. Andrew Marvell: *The Rehearsal Transpros'd*, ed. D.I.B. Smith (OUP 1971) p. 62, quoted Christopher Hill: *The Experience of Defeat* (1984) p. 249: George Wither: *Furor Poeticus* (1660), quoted Christopher Hill: *Collected Essays* Vol. I p. 153.
11. 'But what they killed each for;
    I could not well make out.' Robert Southey: *The Battle of Blenheim*; Sir Edward Dering, quoted Christopher Hill: *Century of Revolution* (1961) p. 125.
12. Christopher Hill: *God's Englishman* (1970) p. 213.
13. John Aubrey: *Brief Lives* (Penguin edtn 1949) p. 36; J. Frank: *The Beginnings of the English Newspaper 1620–1660* (Harvard

UP) pp. 165–6; H.N. Brailsford: *The Levellers and the English Revolution*, ed. Christopher Hill (1961) p. 148.

14. G.E. Aylmer: 'Unbelief in Seventeenth Century England' passim in ed. D. Pennington and Keith Thomas: *Puritans and Revolutionaries* (1978); Thomas Edwards: *Gangraena* Part 1 p. 121 (E323,2); Richard Baxter: *Autobiography*, quoted Woodhouse p. 388; William Dell: *The Building and Glory of the Truly Christian and Spiritual Church* (E363,2).
15. Woodhouse op. cit. p. 102; *Killing No Murder* op. cit p. 393.
16. Blair Worden: 'Classical Republicanism and the Puritan Revolution' p. 182 in ed. H. Lloyd-Jones, V. Pearl and B. Worden: *History and Imagination* (1981); essays presented to H.R. Trevor-Roper (1981); *Past and Present* No. 164 (1999); S.D. Glover: 'The Putney Debates and Elitist Republicanism' p. 59; Woodhouse op. cit. pp. 59, 61.
17. Michael Foot's phrase applied to Tom Paine's *Rights of Man* see *TLS* 26 May 1995.

PART 1 Thomas Rainborough

1. Thomas Rainborough's probable date of birth has been calculated from the likely age on marriage of his father, William, born 1587, and the fact that the third child of that marriage, Martha, was baptised in April 1617, see parish registers St John, Wapping and St Mary, Whitechapel; Boyd's Marriage Index Middlesex Q–Z Misc. 1626.
2. Clarendon Vol. IV p. 331; Gibson Navy Papers BL Add Mss 11, 602f39; Aubrey p. 336; Richard Elton: *The Compleat Body of the Art Military* (1650) chap. XVII.
3. Regimental Banners Temp. Chas I Sloane MS 5247f76; Edward Peacock, 'Notes on the Life of Thomas Rainborough' Appendix B in *Archaeologia* 46 (1876); ed. H.G Tibbutt: *The Letter Books of Sir Samuel Luke* (1963) p. 324.
4. J.R. MacCormack: 'The Irish Adventurers and the English War' in *Irish Historical Studies* Vol. X 1956–1957; L.J. Vol. IV p. 658.
5. Hugh Peter: *True Relation of God's Providence in Ireland*, 18 Nov. 1642 (E242,15).
6. ed. Frances and Margaret Verney: *The Memoirs of the Verney Family* (Tabard Press 1970) Vol. II p. 135.

7. Morton: Ranters pp. 186–187; Brian Manning: 1649 The Crisis of the English Revolution (1992) pp. 187–188,
8. J.R. Powell: *The Navy in the English Civil War* (1962) pp. 21, 48.
9. A.M.W. Stirling: *The Hothams of Hull* (1918) Vol. I pp. 64–5.
10. C.J. Vol. III p. 302; Portland Manuscripts (HMC 13th Rpt, App pt. i) (1891) Vol. I p. 138.
11. Clive Holmes: *The Eastern Association in the English Civil War* (1974) passim and esp. p. 176.
12. Ian Gentles: 'The Iconography of Revolution: England 1642–1649' in ed. Ian Gentles, John Morrill and Blair Worden: *Soldiers, Writers and Statesmen of the English Revolution* (CUP 1998) p. 93.
13. John Vicars: *Magnalia Dei Anglicana or England's Parliamentary Chronicle* Part 4 p. 76.
14. Woolrych pp. 14–16; R.K.G. Temple: 'Original Officer List in the New Model Army' in *The Bulletin of the Institute of Historical Research* No. 59. (1986.)
15. Mark A. Kishlansky: *The Rise of the New Model Army* (Cambridge 1979) p. 46.
16. J.P. Kenyon: *The Civil Wars of England* (1986) p. 141.
17. Austin Woolrych: *Battles of the Civil War* (1961); Sprigge pp. 33–45.
18. Abbott Vol. I p. 376.
19. CJ Vol. IV p. 471; *A Continuation of certain special and remarkable passages informed to Parliament* (E327,4)
20. ed. Henry Cary: *Memorials of the Great Civil War* (1842) p. 221.
21. Sprigge op. cit. opposite p. 334.
22. David Underdown: 'Party Management in the Recruiter Elections 1645–1648' in E.H.R. No. 88 April 1968; David Norbrook: *Writing the Republic* (CUP 1999) p. 147.
23. Clarendon Vol. III pp. 202–9, 216–7; Margaret A. Judson: *The Political Thought of Sir Harry Vane the Younger* (University of Pennsylvania Press 1969) p. 8.
24. Clarendon MS 2,522.
25. CJ Vol. V p. 153; LJ Vol. IX p. 180.
26. Woolrych: pp. 28–30; 'Neat plan' is an expression of J.P. Kenyon's.
27. *The Souldiers Catechisme composed for Parliament's Armies* 1644.
28. *An Apollogie of the Soldiers to all their Commission Officers* (E381,TE); Woolrych p. 35.

29. Woolrych p. 36; Gentles p. 151.
30. Patricia Crawford: *Denzil Holles* (1979) pp. 143–4.
31. Gentles p. 165.
32. ed. J.M. Lloyd Thomas: The Autobiography of Richard Baxter (1925) pp. 49–50; Clarke Vol. I p. 213.
33. Clarke Vol. I pp. x–xi; Morton: Freedom pp. 87–99.
34. John Lilburne: *Jonah's Cry out of the Whale's Belly* (E400,5); *A New Found Stratagem* (E384,11). (This is very probably, if not certainly, by Overton.)
35. CJ Vol. IV p. 153.
36. For the history of the General Council of the Army and its titles see Woolrych pp. 120–1.
37. Clarke Vol. I pp. 22–4, 100.
38. Clarke Vol. I pp.105–6; The Cullum Letter Tanner MS Vol. 58 I fol. 25.
39. Maseres: p. 239; Clarke Vol. I p. 83.
40. Charles Carlton: *Charles I* (1984 paperback edtn) pp. 315–6; Gentles p. 170; Clarke Vol. I p. xxxi.
41. Woodhouse pp. 401–3; The woodcut is the frontispiece to the *Army Book of Declarations* (E409,25). It should be noted that Austin Woolrych does not accept it as a representation of the General Council: Ian Gentles and Gerald Aylmer do.
42. Abbott Vol. I p. 460.
43. Woodhouse pp. 421, 412.
44. Gentles pp. 185–9.
45. Maseres: *Memoirs of Sir John Berkeley* p. 368.
46. For Henry Cholmley's letter see p. 67; Ian Gentles: 'The Struggle for London in the Second Civil War' in the *Historical Journal* XXVI (1983).
47. Berkeley *Memoirs* op. cit. p. 369.
48. Captain Thomas Juxon of the London Militia quoted in Mark A. Kishlansky: *Rise of the New Model Army* op. cit. p. 270.
49. Daniel Lysons: *Environs of London* Vol. II p. 345.
59. ed. H.G. Tibbutt: *The Tower of London Letter-Book of Sir Lewis Dyve* (The Bedfordshire Historical Record Society Vol. 38 1958) pp. 84–5; *The Diary of John Evelyn* (Everyman paperback edtn 1966) p. 268.
51. Berkeley *Memoirs* op. cit. p. 385; Ford to Hopton in Clarendon MS2597 20 Sept. 1647.
52. Capp p. 15; Clarendon Vol. IV p. 332.
53. Dyve op. cit. pp. 84–5, 89–90; J.R. Powell: *Robert Blake:*

General-at-Sea (1976) pp. 70–1; Radicals Dict: Vol. I p. 218; CJ Vol. V p. 312.

54. Dyve op. cit. p. 91; Maseres: *Sundry Reasons inducing Major Robert Huntingdon to lay down his Commission*, p. 403–5.

55. *The Case of the Army*, see Woodhouse pp. 429–36; On the question of Sexby's authorship see a forthcoming essay by Professor John Morrill with Phil Baker on *The Case of the Army Truly Stated*.

56. The first *Agreement of the People* in Morton: Freedom pp. 139–41.

57. *Mercurius Pragmaticus* 11–18 April 1648 (E435,42).

58. Woodhouse p. 14.

59. Woodhouse p. 46; Woolrych p. 232.

60. Woodhouse p. 52.

61. Woodhouse pp. 53, 55–6, 61.

62. Woodhouse p. 87.

63. Woodhouse p. 452.

64. Dyve op. cit. pp. 95–6; Woodhouse p. 55; Woolrych p. 260.

65. Clarke Vol. I p. 413; *A Remonstrance from Sir Thomas Fairfax and his council of War* (E414,14). John Morrill: 'King Killing: No Murder' in *Cromwelliana* 1998 p. 12.

66. *His Majesty's Declaration left by him at Hampton Court* (E413,15); CJ Vol. V p. 357.

67. LJ Vol. IX p. 527; CJ Vol. V pp. 366, 378.

68. Clarendon State Papers Vol. II Appendix p. xli; Clarendon MS 2651.

69. Murray Tolmie: *The Triumph of the Saints* (CUP, 1977) pp. 181–4.

70. Abbott Vol. I pp. 575, 507; CJ Vol. V pp. 312, 403; Thurloe: Vol. I p. 96.

71. Capp op. cit. pp. 15, 17; A.M. Everitt: *The Community of Kent and the Great Rebellion 1640–1660* (Leicester University Press 1966) p. 250.

72. Capp op. cit. p. 16; J.R. Powell and E.K. Timings: *Documents relating to the Civil War 1642–1648* (Naval Records Society No. 105 1963) p. 296.

73. Matthew Carter: *A Most True and exact Relation of that as Honourable as unfortunate Expedition of Kent, Essex and Colchester* (printed 1650).

74. Powell Docs. op. cit. pp. 308, 328; *Dictionary of National Biography*: Lucy Hay, Countess of Carlisle.

75. Carter op. cit. p. 32; Peacock op. cit. p. 37.

76. Powell Docs. op. cit. p. 333; Capp: pp. 20, 30, 45–6; Clarendon Vol. IV p. 404.
77. Gardiner HCW Vol. IV pp. 116–20.
78. Carter op. cit. passim; Rushworth Vol. VII pp. 1150–1243; 'The Siege of Colchester' in *The Antiquary* Vol. I (1880); *The History and Antiquities of Colchester* (1789).
79. Rushworth Vol. VII pp. 1169, 1176.
80. *The Moderate Intelligencer* No. 173 6–13 July 1648 (E452,23).
81. Rushworth Vol. VII p. 1217; J.H. Round: 'The Tower Guards 1648' in *The Antiquary* Vol. X (1884).
82. Rushworth Vol. VII p. 1236.
83. Rushworth Vol. VII p. 1242.
84. 'The Siege of Colchester' in *The Antiquary* Vol. I p. 163.
85. Idem; Up to date information with regard to the site supplied to the author by Mr and Mrs Henry Savill.
86. ed C.H. Firth: *Memoirs of Edmund Ludlow* 2 Vols. (1894) p. 103; Clarke Vol. II pp. 37–8, 86.
87. *Mercurius Melancholicus* 14th–21st Nov. 1648 (E472,26); 'Colonel Rainborough's Ghost' in ed. Thomas Wright: *Early English Poetry and Ballads* (1841).
88. *The Bloody Project* in Morton: Freedom pp. 165–79.
89. Gardiner HCW Vol. IV p. 210; Ludlow *Memoirs* op. cit pp. 262–3.
90. *An Apology unto the honourable and other honoured and worthy officers of His Excellency the Lord General's Army* 4 May 1649. (E552,28).
91. Dyve op. cit. p. 95.
92. Woodhouse pp. 50, 55 and 102.
93. Rushworth Vol. VII pp. 1271, 1279, and 1294.
94. Rushworth Vol. VII p. 1314.
95. Rushworth Vol. VII pp. 1300, 1305 and 1310.
96. Tanner MS 58 f 346 quoted Woolrych pp. 150–1.
97. HMC *Report on the Manuscripts of F.W. Leyborne-Popham Esq. of Littlecote, Wiltshire* pp. 7, 8; *The Moderate* 31 Oct.–7 Nov. 1648 (E470,12).
98. Peacock in *Archaeologia* 46 op. cit. p. 47.
99. *The Moderate* op. cit. (E470,12).
100. Idem.
101. John Lilburne: *England's New Chains Discovered* Part 2 (E458,16).
102. Maurice Ashley: *Cromwell's Generals* (1954) p. 103.

103. Surtees Society Publications Vol. XI (1861); *The Innocent Cleared: or the Vindication of Captain John Smith* (E472,25).
104. *Mercurius Militaris* 14–21 Nov. 1648 (E473,8); *Mercurius Elencticus* 15–22 Nov. 1648 (E473,9).
105. Thomas Brooks: *The Glorious Day of the Saints Appearance*.
106. Elegy (669f13,40).
107. CJ Vol. VI p. 429; ed. Henry Cary: *Memorials of the Great Civil War* Vol. I p. 221; Maurice Ashley: John Wildman (1947) p. 73; ed. H.F. Walters: *The Rainborowe Family* (privately printed NY 1886).

PART 2 Robert Lockyer

1. *Address to Thomas, Lord Fairfax* 27 April 1649 (E552,11).
2. Murray Tolmie: *The Triumph of the Saints* (CUP 1977) p. 156; John Stow: *The Survey of London* (Everyman paperback edtn 1970) p. 149; *Mercurius Pragmaticus* No. 9 (E414,15 & 16).
3. A.A. Cooper, Earl of Shaftesbury in Bishop Burnet: *History of my Own Times* (1823) Vol. I Bk. 11 Chap. 1, note by Onslow p. 164.
4. Laurence Clarkson: *The Lost Sheep Found* (1660) passim; Thomas Edwards: *Gangraena* part 1 p. 63 (E323,2); The Book of Revelation esp. Chaps 13 v18, 20 v20 passim; Daniel Chap. 7 v. 18.
5. Tolmie op. cit. pp. 7–28, 156.
6. William Walwyn: *The Compassionate Samaritane* in Wootton pp. 266, 268; J.F. Wilson: *Pulpit in Parliament* (1969) p. 92.
7. ed. J.M. Lloyd Thomas: *The Autobiography of Richard Baxter* (1925) pp. 49–50.
8. Baxter op. cit. Chap. V.
9. Firth and Davies: pp. 209–30; Gentles p. 199; Woolrych pp. 203, 301–2.
10. *The Army's Martyr* 7 May 1649 (E554,6); C.H. Firth: *Cromwell's Army* (University paperback 1962) p. 405.
11. Woolrych op. cit. Chap. 13.
12. *The Petition of 11 September 1648* in Morton: Freedom pp. 185–94.
13. Gentles op. cit. pp. 287–93; The Whitehall Debates in Woodhouse pp. 125–78.
14. *England's New Chains Discovered* in W. Haller and Davies: *The*

Leveller Tracts 1647–1653 (Columbia UP 1944) pp. 156–89; idem *Picture of the Council of State* p. 204.
15. *The Hunting of the Foxes* (E548,7).
16. *A True Narrative of the Late Mutiny ... in Col Whalley's regiment* (E552,18).
17. *The Justice of the Army against Evill-Doers Vindicated.* (E558,14).
18. Idem; *The Army's Martyr* op. cit.
19. *Declaration of Whalley and all Officers and Soldiers of his Regiment* (E555,31); Firth and Davies: p. 230.
20. *The Moderate* 24 April–1st May (E552,20).
21. Sir William Dugdale's Diary 1649 (unpublished).
22. *Copy of a Letter from Lilburne and Overton to the General* 4 May 1649 (E554,6); *A Petition of Women* 5 May 1649 in Woodhouse p. 367; Gentles p. 316.
23. *A True Narrative* op. cit.

PART 3 William Rainborough

1. H.F. Waters: *The Rainborowe Family* (New York 1886); James Savage: *Genealogical Dictionary of the first Settlers of New England* (Boston 1860).
2. *The Winthrop Papers* Vol. III p. 190; David Cressy: *Coming Over* (CUP 1987) p. 201.
3. J.R. MacCormack: 'The Irish Adventurers and the English Civil War' in *Irish Historical Studies* Vol. X 1956–1957; Boyd's Marriage Index Ipswich,Suffolk A–K 1626–1650.
4. R.P. Stearns: *The Strenuous Puritan* (1954).
5. Firth and Davies pp. 417–18; ed. J.K. Hosmer: *Winthrop's Journal* Vol. II; Waters op. cit.
6. Gardiner, HCW Vol. I p. 225.
7. Woolrych pp. 15–17; L.J. Vol. VII p. 270.
8. Clements R. Markham: *A Life of the Great Lord Fairfax*, battle plans facing pp. 213 and 243.
9. Woolrych pp. 61–3; H.M.C. Portland Vol. III p. 156.
10. *Army Book of Declarations* (E409,25).
11. Clarke Vol. I pp. 45–79.
12. Firth and Davies pp. 175–200; Gentles p. 173.
13. Gentles p. 199; Clarke Vol. I p. 299; Ireton has been described as 'finding the red herring of the franchise' at Putney (Mark A.

Kishlansky: 'The Army and the Levellers: The Roads to Putney', *The Historical Journal* Vol. 22 1979). So far as Radicals were concerned, the franchise issue was far from being a 'red herring' but central to the question of the propertyless individual, dear to both Rainboroughs.

14. Clarke Vol. I pp. 280–363 esp. pp. 299 and 363 for William Rainborough's speeches.

15. Clarke pp. 413–14.

16. Gentles p. 223.

17. Gentles p. 233; Charles Carlton: *Charles I* (Paperback edtn 1984) pp. 342–3.

18. Thomas Brooks: *The Glorious Day of the Saints Appearance*; John Lilburne: *England's New Chains Discovered* (Second Part) (E458,16).

19. William Rainborough's banner in Dr William's Library Modern Folio MS 7 fo 115. (I owe this reference initially to Dr Ian Roy), the banner has been reproduced in ed. Ian Gentles, John Morrill and Blair Worden: *Soldiers, Writers and Statesmen of the English Revolution* (CUP 1998) facing p. 109, also see pp. 97, 108; S.D. Glover: 'The Putney Debates: Popular and Elitist Republicanism' in *Past and Present 1999* No. 164.

20. Gentles pp. 331–48; C.S.P.D. Charles II 1660–1661 p. 416. The 'whiff of grapeshot' comment was made by A.L. Rowse, see *The Regicides* (1994) p. 164.

21. Capp pp. 119, 156; NMMAGC/12/1.

22. Murray Tolmie: *The Triumph of the Saints* (CUP 1977) pp. 181–4; *The Pictures of the Councel of State*: Overton's Narrative in Morton: Freedom p. 201; *The True Levellers' Standard Advanced* in ed. Christopher Hill: *Winstanley: 'The law of Freedom and other Writings'* (CUP 1983) p. 75.

23. Romans 14 v. 14 quoted by Laurence Clarkson in *A Single Eye* in ed. Nigel Smith: *A Collection of Ranter Writings* (1983) p. 170; ed. J.M. Lloyd Thomas: *The Autobiography of Richard Baxter* (1925) p. 73; Christopher Hill: *A Turbulent, Seditious and Factious People* (OUP 1988) p. 81.

24. Smith: *Ranter Writings* op. cit. pp. 8, 13.

25. Laurence Clarkson: *The Lost Sheep Found* (extract) in Smith op. cit. p. 179; Christopher Hill: *The English Bible and the Seventeenth Century Revolution* (1993) p. 18.

26. Laurence Clarkson: *The Lost Sheep Found* (1660).

27. Keith Thomas: 'The Puritans and Adultery: the Act of 1650

Reconsidered' in ed Donald Pennington and Keith Thomas: *Puritans and Revolutionaries* (1978) pp. 257–282.

28. Gardiner HCP Vol. I p. 395; Christopher Hill: *The World Turned Upside Down* (1972) p. 168.
29. Morton: Ranters pp. 135–6.
30. Lawrence Stone: *The Family, Sex and Marriage* (Penguin edtn 1979) p. 315.
31. Clarke Vol. III p. 210.
32. Radicals Dictionary Vol. I pp. 200–01.
33. Christopher Hill: *The Experience of Defeat* (1984) pp. 286–7.
34. C.H. Firth: *Cromwell's Army* (Paperback edtn 1962) pp. 5, 17; *The Experience of Defeat* op. cit. p. 284; CJ Vol. VII pp. 723, 753.
35. Capp p. 342 footnote; *The Remonstrance and Protestation of the Well-Affected People* first published in Edinburgh 1660 (NB very difficult to read) 669f22,11.
36. Clarendon Vol. VI p. 234; Christopher Hill: *A Century of Revolution* (1961) p. 189.
37. C.S.P.D. Ch. II 1660–1661 pp. 416, 450; Pepys Vol. I pp. 120, 127; Edmund Ludlow: *A Voice from the Watch Tower* Part 5 ed. Blair Worden (1978) p. 275; R.L. Greaves: *Deliver Us from Evil* (OUP 1986) pp. 35–40, 83–4.

PART 4 Edward Sexby

1. Clarendon Vol. VI p. 80.
2. S.D. Glover: 'The Putney Debates: Popular and Elitist Republicanism' in Past and Present 1999 No. 164 passim; *Killing No Murder* in Wootton p. 367; Blair Worden: *Classical Republicanism and the Puritan Revolution* in ed. Hugh Lloyd-Jones, Valerie Pearl, and Blair Worden: History and Imagination, (1981); David Norbrook: *Writing the Republic* (CUP 1999) p. 34.
3. Professor John Morrill with Phil Baker: *The Case of the Armie Truly Stated* in a collection of essays about Putney due out in early 2001. Brian Manning: *The English People and the English Revolution* (Penguin edtn 1978) p. 107; Richard Grasby: 'Social Mobility and Business Enterprise in Seventeenth Century England' in ed. Donald Pennington and Keith Thomas: *Puritans and Revolutionaries* (1978).
4 G. Unwin: *The Gilds and Companies of London* (1908) p. 335; *A Remonstrance from Sir Thomas Fairfax* (E414,14); Woolrych

194

p. 287; C.H. Firth: *Cromwell's Army* (University paperback 1962) p. 274.

5. Fairfax's letter quoted in Mark Kishlansky: *Rise of the New Model Army* (CUP 1979) p. 64.
6. John Lilburne: *Jonah's Cry out of the Whale's Belly* (E400,5).
7. Ibid; P. Gregg: *Free-born John* (1967) p. 163.
8. *An Apollogie of the Souldiers to all their Commission Officers in Sir Thomas Fairfax his Army* (E381,18); H.M.C. Portland Vol. III p. 156. *The Apologie of the Common Soldiers to the General* (E385,18).
9. *The Vindication of the Officers presented to the Commons* (E385,19); *Apollogie* op. cit. (E381,18).
10. Clarke Vol. I pp. 430–1.
11. Ibid; Gentles p. 160.
12. Clarke Vol. I pp. 82, 86.
13. Rushworth Vol. I p. 485; Woolrych pp. 75, 129, 149.
14. Woolrych pp. 132–3, 302; Gentles p. 176; Thoresby Record Society XI pp. 143, 155, 167 and 191.
15. Clarke Vol. I pp. 148, 207.
16. Clarke Vol. I p. 171; Gentles p. 199; Woolrych pp. 191–2, 203.
17. ed. H.G. Tibbutt: *The Tower of London Letter-Book of Sir Lewis Dyve* (Bedfordshire Historical Record Society Vol. 38 1958) p. 92.
18. Gentles p. 204.
19. Clarke Vol. I p. 226.
20. Clarke Vol. I pp. 226–406. (Cromwell's speech recorded on p.328 accusing Sexby of 'will' seems to refer to a speech of Sexby's which William Clarke missed. Sexby's next recorded speech apologises for 'zeal' but confirms that he is not sorry for having spoken what he conceived to be the truth.)
21. Jeremiah 51 v. 9; Christopher Hill: *The English Bible in the Seventeenth-Century* (1993) p. 112: Woodhouse pp. 102–3.
22. Clarke Vol. I pp. 407–9; Woodhouse pp. 452–4.
23. Clarke Vol. I pp. 412–14.
24. *A Declaration of Some Proceedings of Lt. Col John Lilburne* in *The Leveller Tracts 1647–1653* ed. W. Haller and G. Davies (Columbia UP 1944) p. 123.
25. Gentles pp. 245–6.
26. *The Bloody Project* (unsigned but generally agreed to be by William Walwyn) in Morton: Freedom pp. 161, 169.
27. Clarke Vol. II pp. 254–5.
28. C.J. Vol. V p. 680.

29. Gardiner HCP Vol. I pp. 24, 30–1, 34; Clarke Vol. II p. 193. James Holstun: *Ehud's Dagger: Class Struggle in the English Revolution* (Verso 2000) p. 309.
30. Clarke MS xix fol. 26–27 in Worcester College Library, Oxford; G.E. Aylmer: *The State's Servants* (1973) pp. 155–6: C.H. Firth: *Cromwell's Army* op. cit. pp. 303–4; Austin Woolrych: *Commonwealth to Protectorate* (1982) p. 259.
31. Clarke Vol. III p. xvi; Gardiner HCP Vol. II pp. 92–3.
32. Philip A. Knachel: *England and the Fronde* (Cornel UP 1967) pp. 41–2, 180; *The Hunting of the Foxes* (E548,7).
33. Knachel p. 197; H.N. Brailsford: *The Levellers and the English Revolution* (1961) pp. 671–92; Timothy Venning: *Cromwellian Foreign Policy* (1995) p.42; David Norbrook: *Writing the Republic* (CUP 1998) p. 224; *Mercurius Politicus* no. 1 (E603,6).
34. Abbott Vol. III p. 272; ed. C.H. Firth: *The Journal of Joachim Hane* (1856).
35. Brailsford op. cit. p. 687. Holstun p. 310.
36. Clarke Vol. III p. 197.
37. L.F. Ellis: *Victory in the West* Vol. I p. 144 (1960).
38. Capp p. 88.
39. Abbott Vol. IV p. 268; *The Hunting of the Foxes* (extract) Morton: Freedom p. 149; Woodhouse pp. 7, 197.
40. Daniel Chap. 7 passim; Revelation 13 v. 18; H.R. Trevor-Roper: *Religion, the Reformation and Social Change* (1967).
41. Gardiner HCP Vol. III pp. 69, 73; Abbott Vol. III p. 435.
42. Thurloe Vol. III pp. 162, 165, 194–5; Ashley pp. 102–3; Gardiner HCP pp. 117, 119f; Holstun pp. 216, 353.
43. Nicholas Papers Vol. II pp. 299, 340, Vol. III p. 15.
44. Nicholas Papers Vol. III pp. 2, 176.
45. Ibid. pp. 118, 128; Clarendon State Papers Vol. III pp. 311, 312, 339.
46. Ashley pp. 98–9,112.
47. C.H. Firth: *Last Years of the Protectorate* Vol. I (1909) p. 34f.
48. Ibid. p. 37; Clarendon State Papers Vol. III p. 331.
49. Thurloe Vol. V pp.774–7, Vol. VI pp. 693–4.
50. *State Trials* Vol. V pp. 845, 858.
51. *Killing No Murder* in Wootton pp. 360–88; Firth Vol. I p. 222 for the authorship controversy.
52. Clarendon State Papers Vol. III pp. 335, 338; Clarke III p. 114.
53. Abbott Vol. IV p. 647; Olivier Lutaud: Des Révolutions d'Angleterre à la Révolutions Française (The Hague 1973) pp. 93–4.

PART 5 Richard Rumbold

1. *State Trials* Vol. XI pp. 874–87.
2. Clarke Vol. I pp. 193–4; *The Hunting of the Foxes* March 1649 (E548,7).
3. G.E. Aylmer: 'Locke no Leveller' in ed. Ian Gentles, John Morrill and Blair Worden: *Soldiers, Writers and Statesmen of the English Revolution*; (CUP 1998) p. 314.
4. C.J. Vol. VII p. 698; *State Trials* Vol. XI p. 822: *State Trials* Vol. IX pp. 306, 401; BL Add Mss 38, 847 f88; Edmund Ludlow: *A Voyce from the Watch Tower* Part 5, ed. Blair Worden (1978) pp. 11–12.
5. 'Locke no Leveller' op. cit. p.308; Peter Earle: *Monmouth's Rebels* (1977) p. 192; K.H.D. Haley: *The First Earl of Shaftesbury* (Clarendon Press, Oxford 1968) p. 716.
6. BI Add Mss 38, 847 f88; John Dryden: *Absalom and Achitophel* 1.1.224–5; *Cromwelliana*, The Journal of the Cromwell Association (1999). Address by Roy Sherwood, who explains that Cromwell had ordered two caps of state, traditionally worn by kings as badges of rank in place of a crown, shortly before his death.
7. R.L. Greaves: *Secrets of the Kingdom* (Stanford 1992) p. 331; BL Add Mss 38, 847 f88.
8. Haley op. cit. p. 709; Greaves op. cit. p. 116.
9. J.P. Kenyon: *The Popish Plot* (1972); Alan Marshall: *The Strange Death of Edmund Godfrey* (2000).
10. Greaves op. cit. p. 7.
11. David Ogg: *England in the Reign of Charles II* (OUP 1934) Vol. II pp. 618–19.
12. J.P. Kenyon: *The Popish Plot* (1972) p. 33; Greaves op. cit. p. 145.
13. James Ferguson: *Robert Ferguson The Plotter* (Edinburgh State Trials) Vol. IX pp.406, 527.
14. BL Add Mss 38847,f88 et. seq.; Greaves op. cit. p. 117; *State Trials* Vol. IX p. 401.
15. Greaves op. cit. pp. 146, 257; BL Add Mss op. cit.; *State Trials* Vol. IX p. 405.
16. Greaves op. cit. p. 147; J.P. Hore: *History of Newmarket and Annals of the Turf* Vol. III (1886) p. 64.
17. Hore op. cit. p. 69; Greaves p. 154.
18. Greaves p. 181.

19. Ferguson op. cit. p. 434; BL Add MSS op. cit.; Macaulay: *History of England* (1895) Vol. I p. 256.
20. *State Trials* Vol. IX op. cit. p. 410; Greaves pp. 189–92.
21. PRO SP 29/430/pt1; Greaves p. 188.
22. John Willcock: *A Scots Earl in Covenanting Times* (1907) passim; Macaulay op. cit. pp. 91, 262.
23. Robin Clifton: *The Last Popular Rebellion* (1984) p. 150.
24. Willcock op. cit.; Clifton op. cit. p. 155.
25. *State Trials* Vol. X pp. 874–87.
26. Ferguson p. 134.

EPILOGUE

1. Cromwell's *Soldier's Bible*, a reprint in facsimile, Pryor Publications, 1997, obtainable from the Cromwell Association; Christopher Hill: *The Bible in the Seventeenth Century* (1993), pp. 56–66.

APPENDIX A

In connection with the subject of these banners I have received much help and information from Ian Gentles' essay 'The iconography of the Revolution: England 1642–1649' in ed. Ian Gentles, John Morrill and Blair Worden: *Soldiers, Writers and Statesmen of the English Revolution, Essays presented to Austin Woolrych* (CUP, 1998).

1. Alan R. Young: *The English Emblem Tradition*, 111, Emblematic Flag Devices of the English Civil Wars 1642–1660.
2. Thomas Blount: *The Art of Making Devises* (1648); Turmile MS (MS12.7) also known as Modern Folio MS7f115; BL Sloane MS 5247f76.
3. Blount p. 79; Turmile pp. 117 and 79.
4. Sloane MS op. cit.

APPENDIX B The Rye House Plot

1. *State Trials* Vol. IX p. 519; Bishop Burnett: *History of his own Time* (1823) Vol. II p. 349; R.L. Greaves: *Secrets of the Kingdom* (Stamford University Press 1992) p. 206; J.R. Dinwiddy: *Radicalism and Reform in Britain 1780–1850* (Hambledon Press 1992) p. 20.
2. *State Trials* op. cit. pp. 353–36, and esp. p. 602.
3. James Ferguson: *Robert Ferguson The Plotter* (Edinburgh 1887) p. 259.
4. J.P. Hore: *History of Newmarket and Annals of the Turf* Vol. III (1886) p. 69; PRO 29/423/Pt2.

INDEX

201

204